PIPPA GREENWOOD
FLOWER
GARDENER

PIPPA GREENWOOD
FLOWER GARDENER

DORLING KINDERSLEY
LONDON • NEW YORK • SYDNEY • MOSCOW

A DORLING KINDERSLEY BOOK

*To Callum, who was with me every minute that this
book was being written and was born just as it
was going to press, with lots of love*

PROJECT EDITORS
Jennifer Jones & Annabel Morgan

ART EDITOR
Jane Bull

DTP DESIGNER
Matthew Greenfield

MANAGING EDITOR
Louise Abbott

MANAGING ART EDITOR
Lee Griffiths

SPECIAL PHOTOGRAPHY
Dave King

PRODUCTION
Silvia La Greca

PICTURE RESEARCH
Sean Hunter

Copyright © 1998
Dorling Kindersley Limited, London
Text copyright © 1998 Pippa Greenwood

First published in Great Britain in 1998 by
Dorling Kindersley Limited, 9 Henrietta Street, London WC2 8PS
Visit us on the World Wide Web at http://www.dk.com

2 4 6 8 10 9 7 5 3 1

A CIP catalogue record for this book is available from the British Library

ISBN 0 7513 0613 4

Reproduction by GRB, Italy
Printed and bound in China by Imago

Contents

INTRODUCTION *6*

Introduction

WHETHER YOU ARE A NEW GARDENER OR AN OLD ONE, NOVICE OR EXPERT, IT IS FLOWERING PLANTS THAT ARE MOST LIKELY TO BRING YOUR GARDEN TO LIFE, NO MATTER WHAT ITS SIZE, ASPECT, SOIL TYPE OR DIFFICULT FEATURES. WHETHER USED AS THE LIVING THREADS in a border tapestry, or viewed close-up in a tub or vase, they never fail to lift the spirits. And even though I've lived and worked among flowers all my life, each year their sheer beauty, variety and complexity of form still take my breath away. It's almost impossible to pick out my favourites – but I have, I hope, made a selection here that even the newest gardener will find easy to grow, and picked out varieties that will be easy to find – although a helpful nursery or garden centre will always be able to recommend alternatives, if necessary. Whether you have gardened for years, or only recently started to try your hand at it, flower gardening is guaranteed to bring you immense pleasure and satisfaction. I hope that this book will inspire and encourage you to get out into the garden and make the very most of your own special patch.

Pippa Greenwood

GARDENING

WITH

FLOWERS

What is a flower?

FLOWERS LOOK — and smell — the way they do for one compelling reason: to reproduce. To set seed they must be pollinated, and with their flowers they attract insects that will bear pollen from flower to flower, and plant to plant. We group plants that will cross-pollinate and reproduce together into "species"; as in the animal kingdom, breeding between species often produces sterile plants — think of a mule. Within a species, natural genetic variation may act to produce, say, different flower colours, just as families have blue- and brown-eyed children. If a breeder can propagate an attractive variant so as to guarantee it will appear in the plant, it may be sold as a "named variety".

STEP INSIDE
Bees rummaging in flowers pick up a dusting of pollen on their furry bodies — they're the perfect vehicle for transporting pollen from flower to flower.

CLEARED FOR LANDING
As clearly marked as runways for aeroplanes, the dark "guidelines" on the petals of this pansy lead pollinators straight in.

Pollen packed on stamens needs to reach the stigma in the centre — usually, of another flower

Flowers open in succession, ensuring that pollination occurs over a long period

Colours in the red-blue range have insect appeal

BEAUTY PARLOUR
With its beautiful colour and scent, this lily has considerable insect allure — its open shape and prominent stamens ensure each visit is a "hit".

TUNNEL VISION
It's a tight squeeze to reach the nectar at the end of penstemons' funnel-shaped flowers, cosy enough to cover any visiting insect liberally with a generous coating of pollen.

HIDDEN ATTRACTIONS
Flowers like miniature lidded "suitcases" ensure that the pollen and nectar of lupins are well protected from the weather, while easily tipping open under the weight of pollinating insects.

HITTING THE SPOT

Centre strongly marked

Butterflies love to land, feed and bask on flat flowers: like the bull's-eye on a target, the centre of this anemone guides them in.

Showy bracts surround tiny flowers

POLLINATING PLOYS

When their flowers are insignificant, as in this euphorbia, plants employ other wiles: scents, for example (not always attractive to us humans!), or, as here, ruffs of showy, leafy bracts that have the same "over here" appeal as petals.

FLOWERING LIFESPANS

Plants vary greatly in their longevity and the time it takes for them to produce flowers, and this is crucial to the way we use them in gardens. Annuals blithely grow from seed, flower, set seed and die in a single season, while perennial plants, with more of an eye to posterity, flower year after year. These plants develop long-term survival strategies – lying safe and dormant below ground during cold winters, for example, or developing robust, permanent woody frameworks – the plants we call shrubs and trees. Many plants, with even more of a "belt and braces" approach to ensuring their survival, have extra, non-sexual ways of reproducing, so they are not completely reliant on setting seed – their roots and stems spread and form new, miniature plantlets, identical to their parent and capable of independent survival. Gardeners have long exploited this potential, not only to make new plants, but also to perpetuate sterile hybrids and to eliminate the possibility of natural variation in named varieties.

PERENNIAL PERSISTENCE

Perennial plants have the potential to last for many years. Herbaceous perennials like this *Anemone × hybrida* 'Max Vogel' will die back completely in late autumn, then send up new growth again in spring. Evergreen perennials retain their leaves all year.

ANNUAL APPEAL

Annuals complete their entire life cycle in one year, so seed is sown, germinates and produces a plant that flowers, sets seed and then dies all within one year. Here, a glorious, colourful meadow of annuals, including cornflowers, godetia, Californian poppies and daisies provides an easy, low-cost way to produce sensational colour quickly.

TWO-YEAR TENURE

Biennials such as these wallflowers need two growing seasons to complete their life cycle. In the first year, biennial seeds produce a leafy plant, followed by flowers in the second year. Most die or are best removed at the end of the second year. Many biennials can be bought as one-year-old plants, which can be useful if you have limited time or facilities.

The flowering year

THE FLOWER GARDEN AT THE height of summer rarely disappoints – but outside the main season it's often a different story. Yet, with a bit of careful planning, you can create a garden in which new flowers are opening almost all year round, generating a wonderful sense of expectation and pride. And when the flowers of the season invite you so appealingly into the garden to care for them, even your least favourite gardening tasks are a pleasure too.

RITES OF SPRING
Roll out a richly coloured carpet for the arrival of spring with a bed of red and yellow tulips, blue forget-me-nots and rusty red and brown wallflowers. Add a sprinkling of white narcissus and hyacinths, and you have something just as exotic and beautiful as an intricate oriental tapestry, with the bonus of fragrance, too.

EARLY START
That time of the year when spring turns into summer can be a tricky period for colour in the garden – spring flowers have come and gone, but the full glory of the summer is yet to come. Here, a luminous pink lavatera, *Achillea* and some early roses step in to fill the gap beautifully. All of these plants will continue to flower for much of the summer.

TOO HOT TO HANDLE
By mid-summer, plantings should be lush and voluptuous; as the season reaches its height, let baking borders become a tinderbox of colour with fiery dahlias and red-hot pokers, here heightened by the golden yellows and brownish-reds of the daisy-like heleniums in the foreground. This border will still be glowing into autumn.

AUTUMN COLOUR

Proof, if ever it was needed, that autumn has its pleasures, too. This superb planting is simplicity itself, with the pink flowers of colchicum growing through (and supported by) the foliage of hardy geraniums as it starts to develop autumnal reddish tints, adding to the beauty of the display.

SMALL WONDERS

Winter's treasures are mainly small, cool and very elegant. One of the sights I enjoy most at this time of year is a carpet of *Cyclamen coum* in pink or white dotted with dainty posies of the single snowdrop *Galanthus nivalis*. With a planting like this, no one could ever suggest that winter in the garden is boring!

REFLECTED GLORY *right*

The cloudless blue skies of mid-summer are mirrored and amplified to a serene azure in these cornflowers.

A flower garden calendar

SEASON	SPRING	SUMMER
WHAT'S HAPPENING IN THE GARDEN	With the arrival of spring the whole flower garden starts to emerge from its long winter sleep. As temperatures rise and the days become both brighter and longer, vibrant new life is suddenly pumped into the beds and borders and everything starts to put on growth: stems shoot up from the dark soil, buds break and fresh foliage and flowers are produced. In no time at all the gloominess of winter disappears and the garden is studded with the first of the spring flowers.	Summer is a glorious time in the garden, packed to bursting with fast-growing plants covered in flowers. The garden is a hive of activity – both for wildlife and for you. There are lots of jobs to be done at this time, not least a regular patrol of the garden to check for pests and diseases. Towards the end of the summer many flowers are slowing down, producing fewer blooms, so unless it is carefully planned the garden may cease to offer such a breathtaking show.
WHAT'S LOOKING GOOD	Anemones, aubretia, perennial candytuft, forget-me-nots, some heathers, pasque flowers, periwinkles, polyanthus, primulas, veronicas, violas, violets, wallflowers, winter bellis. There's a host of spring-flowering bulbs to enjoy, including bluebells, crocuses, crown imperials, daffodils, grape hyacinths, hyacinths, early irises, snakeshead fritillaries and tulips.	Acanthus, alchemilla, alyssum, anaphalis, aquilegias, arctotis, campanulas, clematis, delphiniums, doronicums, echinops, feverfew, godetia, gypsophila, hebes, helianthemums, hibiscus, irises, larkspur, lavender, lilies, lychnis, meconopsis, mignonette, morning glory, peonies, poppies, stocks, sunflowers, thrift, thyme, verbascums and most of the bedding plants.
WHAT TO DO	• Early in the season, clear borders of the last of the faded stems and foliage from herbaceous perennials. • Plant perennials, especially if you have a heavy soil that makes autumn planting a bit risky. • Get stakes and other plant supports in position for flowers that come into growth early on. • Start to feed plants. Use a high-potash fertilizer to encourage flowers, and a complete fertilizer for boosting overall growth. • Sow seeds – early in spring for annuals and late in the season for hardy perennials. • Plant summer-flowering bulbs such as lilies. • Lift, divide and transplant snowdrops and winter aconites. • As herbaceous perennials start to reshoot from the base, take basal cuttings from suitable plants. • Divide and replant any perennials that are overcrowded. • Keep a look out for pests and diseases and control them before they get a hold. • Prune late-flowering clematis early in spring. • Apply a mulch around the base of perennials.	• Continue to feed flowers regularly. Although annuals can be fed right through until the end of summer, stop feeding perennials after mid-summer. • Early in the season plant autumn-flowering bulbs such as colchicums. • Water as necessary, especially during hot weather and on light soils. • Supply stakes and other supports to perennials before they put on too much growth. • Deadhead flowers frequently, but if you want to save your own seed, remember to allow a few seedheads to develop. • Tie in growth of climbers. • Regularly pick sweet peas to ensure a constant supply. • Early in the season, sow more half-hardy annuals to give colour later in the summer. • Make routine checks for pests and diseases, and take appropriate action if any are found. • Late in the summer collect seeds from favourite flowers. • Sow seeds of perennials. • Sow seeds of biennials where they are to flower next year.

AUTUMN

As the days become shorter and noticeably colder, many plants start to prepare for the winter – growth slows down considerably, especially towards the end of the season. Now is the time to enjoy all the warmth that rudbeckias, sedums, solidago and red-hot pokers can offer. Many flowers that were in bloom earlier in the year now have interesting seedheads, berries or fruits, and their foliage may take on attractive colours as it starts to die back.

Arctotis, asters, cannas, centaurea, Viticella Group clematis, chrysanthemums, colchicums, crocosmias, autumn crocuses, autumn-flowering cyclamen, dahlias, echinaceas, gaillardia, autumn gentians, hebes, heleniums, Japanese anemones, kaffir lilies, nerines, phygelius, red-hot pokers, rudbeckias, sedums, solidago, sternbergia, tiger lilies.

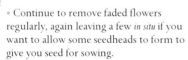

• Continue to remove faded flowers regularly, again leaving a few *in situ* if you want to allow some seedheads to form to give you seed for sowing.
• Plant perennials – autumn is an especially good season for doing this if your soil is on the dry side.
• Clear most of the faded foliage from perennials, although leaving some in position may help to provide protection from winter cold.
• Remove the last of the summer bedding plants and replace them with winter- or spring-flowering bedding to bring you fresh colour.
• Check for the presence of pests and diseases which are capable of surviving over the winter.
• Plant plenty of spring bulbs in borders and in containers, or perhaps even in the lawn.
• Lift gladiolus and dahlia corms and tubers, and store in a dry place.
• Prepare soil for planting later in the autumn or in spring. Dig in some bulky organic matter and apply slow-release fertilizers.
• Lift and divide overcrowded clumps of herbaceous perennials. Replant the new root clumps immediately.

WINTER

In winter the majority of perennials and bulbs become dormant and many of them die back. Consequently, those that do remain in leaf – or, better still, those that come into flower at this time – are real jewels, focal points in what can otherwise be a somewhat bleak patch. With careful planning, you can ensure that there is always something of interest to brighten up the winter garden. Site winter plants close to the house so that you can view them through the window regardless of the weather.

Plants in flower include early crocuses, cyclamen, winter-flowering heathers, hellebores, irises (notably *Iris reticulata* and *I. unguicularis*), leucojums, early narcissus, snowdrops and winter aconites. Many plants such as sedums and thistles look stunning when covered in a hoar frost, provided you have left the dead flower stems in place.

• Well before any cold weather really begins to bite, lift all perennials that will not survive winter outdoors and move them to a frost-free spot, or provide winter protection.
• Continue to clear autumn leaves from around plants before they become soggy and encourage rotting.
• Plan what you want to achieve and grow next year.
• Order seeds from catalogues as soon as possible while the best selection is still available. Store the seeds in a cool but frost-free, dry place until it is time to sow them.

Giving plants a good start

THERE'S NO BIG SECRET to successful gardening – if you get new plants off to a good start, you will find it much easier to keep them healthy and looking good. The first step is to find a reputable supplier – whether a garden centre, nursery or mail-order company. This is essential, as you need to be sure that the plants have been properly grown and looked after before you part with your money. Spend a bit of time deciding where to buy your plants, then which plants to buy, and you can be confident that you have good-quality specimens. The rest – choosing the right site, planting them carefully and nurturing them while they establish – is up to you.

BUYING PERENNIALS
Choose vigorous plants, with healthy, green top growth – no yellowing leaves, wilting or signs of pests and diseases. If you look carefully you may find a real bargain – this primula is ripe for division, and will give me three plants for the price of one.

CHOOSING BEDDING PLANTS
Always choose healthy-looking, sturdy plants with plenty of buds rather than flowers – I'll put back a tray of blooming plants, as they have already used up part of their flowering potential.

PLANTING

Planting is easy, and should be good fun. The steps shown here do not take long and they should ensure that your plants have the best chance of success. Unless you can guarantee that you will look after your plants well, try to buy them as close to planting time as possible, so that there is no risk of them drying out or being damaged before you plant them. If your soil is on the dry side, dig in bulky organic matter before you start. If it tends to hold water rather too well, incorporate garden grit and compost.

1 Dig a planting hole that is wider and deeper than the root ball and loosen the soil around the edges. Sprinkle a complete fertilizer into the soil you have removed and mix in thoroughly.

2 If the compost is dry, water thoroughly first. Grip the pot in one hand and support the crown of the plant in the other. Squeeze the pot to loosen the root ball, then invert it to free the plant.

3 Use your fingertips to loosen up the root ball, gently teasing some of the outer roots free. This ensures that the roots will soon start to explore the soil around the planting hole.

HOW MANY PLANTS?

A wilting plant has either been allowed to get too dry, or overwatered — and perhaps not for the first time. A plant that is repeatedly treated badly will suffer from damage that may not be immediately visible — for example, root death.

Buy from nurseries and garden centres that are tidy and clean; they can usually be relied on to supply healthy plants.

Resist a "bargain" unless you know that you can cope with it — a price-reduced plant is not a good buy if it is going to take too long to recover, or if it brings pest and disease problems.

If you have a favourite garden centre, try to find out when it has its stock delivered — then time your visit so that you can pick up the best and freshest plants.

When shopping for plants, don't forget that the small specimen in front of you may bear no relation to its ultimate size. If you don't want to end up with an overcrowded border, work out first how many plants you will need when they are *fully grown*, or take a notepad with you, plus the dimensions of the border, and check plant labels for their final height and width. If the border looks sparse at first, fill gaps with bedding plants.

PLANTING GROUPS
To work out the spacing between two different types of plant, take the sum of both their spreads and divide by two.

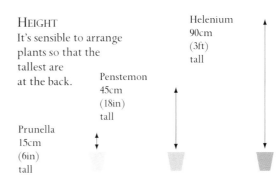

Three heleniums 60cm (2ft) apart as per final spread

Three penstemons 60cm (2ft) apart as per final spread

Three prunellas 45cm (18in) apart as per final spread

PLANT SPREAD
This young penstemon will eventually spread as far as the outer circle.

HEIGHT
It's sensible to arrange plants so that the tallest are at the back.

Helenium 90cm (3ft) tall

Penstemon 45cm (18in) tall

Prunella 15cm (6in) tall

4 Check that the plant is at the correct depth and that the surface of the compost is level with the top of the planting hole. Carefully backfill, firming the soil between the roots and the sides of the hole.

5 Water thoroughly using a watering can. Top up with soil if dents appear, making sure that the plant itself is sitting at the same depth as it was when in its container.

6 Mulch the whole of the root area to deter weeds and help to keep the soil moist. A 5–7.5cm (2–3in) layer works best, spread all around the plant but leaving the area around its stems clear.

Most planting is best carried out in either autumn or spring, but check plant labels for specific advice.

In spring or summer, plant in early evening so that the plant can settle in before being subjected to the heat of the day.

Water the soil well before planting. Never plant in waterlogged or frozen soil. Keep well watered while the plant establishes.

Growing from seed

BY RAISING YOUR OWN FLOWERS from seed, you open up a whole new world of possibilities. The range of plants available is tremendous – far greater than that at a garden centre – and growing from seed is also fun, especially if you start with some of the easier seeds that don't need extra heat to germinate and grow. The low cost of compost and trays or pots means that this way of stocking your garden is very inexpensive. Once you have proved to yourself that you can do it, you might want to invest in a small heated propagator and try some trickier seeds.

Some seed can be sown directly outdoors (see pp.20–21), but the range is far greater if you start seeds under cover, as here. If you don't have a greenhouse, place your pots and trays of seedlings on a sunny windowsill on aluminium foil (for added light reflection) and turn them often so that they grow up straight rather than leaning towards the light. Watering the compost with a copper-based fungicide helps to prevent a disease called damping off.

SOWING UNDER COVER

1 All you need is a seed tray and some multipurpose compost. A new or well-scrubbed tray and bagged, sterile compost reduces the risk of disease. Sieve the compost.

4 Scatter the seeds evenly and thinly over the compost. Try putting the seeds in one cupped hand and gently tapping with the fingers of the other hand to control the flow.

2 Fill the tray to the top. Tamp down the compost and level off, by hand or with a small piece of board. The compost surface should be about 1cm (½in) below the rim of the tray.

3 Use a watering can fitted with a rose to moisten the compost thoroughly. Use mains water, again for good hygiene. If the rose is adjustable, position it so it faces upwards.

5 Most seeds need a fine covering of compost: check the back of the packet. If this is not needed, cover the tray with plastic wrap; this helps to keep seeds moist and lets light in.

SOWING FINE SEEDS

Most seeds are fairly easy to handle, but if they are very fine, like lobelia seeds, they are difficult to distribute thinly enough and so need special care. If you sow seeds too thickly, the resulting seedlings are hard to separate, and they are also very prone to disease and to becoming etiolated (drawn and yellow). Mixing seed with sand is an easy way to "dilute" the seed. You then drizzle this mixture onto the compost to create a more uniform spread.

1 Mix the seeds thoroughly with plenty of horticultural-grade silver sand. Don't be tempted to use cheaper builder's sand, as it may contain impurities that inhibit germination or growth.

2 A piece of stiff paper or cardboard with a central fold makes an excellent chute from which to trickle the seed and sand mixture gently and evenly over the surface of the compost.

SEEDS AND VERMICULITE

Many fine seeds need light to germinate. Cover them with vermiculite (a lightweight granular material), which helps to keep seeds moist and allows some light through.

PRICKING OUT SEEDLINGS

Seedlings need space to grow well, and you will probably need to transfer them ("prick them out") to roomier surroundings as soon as one or two pairs of true leaves have formed. Prepare some small pots or another tray (see opposite). Always water the compost thoroughly before removing seedlings from their tray, as this makes the job easier and reduces the risk of root damage.

1 Carefully ease each seedling out of the tray. I use a pencil, but a dibber is fine too. Take care not to damage the roots, and handle the seedling by its seed leaves.

2 Make regularly spaced holes in the compost of the new tray and carefully lower each seedling into its hole. Firm back around its roots, then water or mist.

PLANTING OUT

Most flower seedlings raised under glass will need to be transplanted ("potted on") again, this time into individual pots. This ensures that each young plant has a well-developed root system and plenty of top growth before it is acclimatized to conditions outdoors, or "hardened off". To harden off, place plants outdoors in a sheltered spot during the day for several days and bring them in at night. Wait until after any late frosts before planting out.

GROWING SEEDS IN CELLS

Large seeds, or the prepared "pelleted" seeds often available for popular plants, can be sown in individual modules or cells. This method of sowing seeds is particularly useful, because it means that they don't need pricking out and when it is time to move them into more spacious surroundings, each seedling has its own well-developed and undisturbed root system.

1 Sieve compost over the surface of the cells and then use your hand to distribute it evenly into the cells so that each is filled to just beneath the rim.

2 Insert each seed – here sunflowers – into a separate cell and cover with compost. You can also sow two seeds to a cell and then thin out the weaker ones.

3 Press the base of each cell to release the neat plug of compost housing a well-developed root system. Pot on or plant out the seedlings as necessary.

GROWING HARDY ANNUALS IN DRIFTS

Not all seed requires an indoor start with trays, pots and compost. Hardy annuals can be sown directly into the garden, either as "fillers" between perennials or, as here, in blocks to create masses of colour. Sowing is generally a spring job, though some plants can be sown in autumn. Look at the back of seed packets to see whether the seed is suitable for outdoor sowing, and to check timing, planting depth and spacing.

1 Clear the bed of weeds, debris and large stones. Dig it over well and make it level. Keeping your feet horizontal, gently tread over the bed to firm the soil and prevent later subsidence.

2 Using a rake, gently loosen the top layer of the soil so that seeds sown have good conditions in which to germinate. If soil needs feeding, incorporate some fertilizer as you do this.

3 Use horticultural-grade sand to mark out the areas into which you will then sow each type of seed (*left*). Uneven-sized patches will look best unless you want to achieve a more formal look. You may need to use the rake to "fluff up" soil that you have knelt on and flattened.

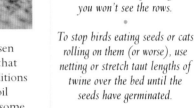

Always use horticultural sand, not builder's sand, which plants hate. Use dry, not moist, sand to work with; it's easier to handle.

•

Seeds sown in straight drills may produce seedlings that look regimented at first, but as you thin them and the plants grow you won't see the rows.

To stop birds eating seeds or cats rolling on them (or worse), use netting or stretch taut lengths of twine over the bed until the seeds have germinated.

5 Sow the seeds along the drills. Don't waste seed by sowing too densely, but always sow more than you need; it's best to have to thin seedlings later.

4 Use a stick or bamboo cane to mark out grooves, or "drills", into which you will sow the seed. Sowing in rows makes it easier to tell weed and flower seedlings apart when they come up.

6 Push the ridges over to cover the seeds with soil. Unless rain is forecast in the next few days, gently water the area. As the seedlings develop, thin out where necessary.

Home-grown seeds

Perennial pea
(*Lathyrus latifolius*)

GROWING FLOWERS FROM SEEDS that you have collected yourself from the garden is always satisfying. Some plants, particularly the species and a few named varieties, will "come true" from seed: their offspring will closely resemble the parent plant. Most named varieties, and anything called an "F1 hybrid", produce plants that are not the same as the parents, but the results of these "pot luck" plants are often very pretty and well worth growing. Never save seed from plants that are diseased, as some infections can be transmitted by seed. Always clearly label what you have collected and when.

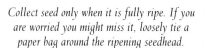

Collect seed only when it is fully ripe. If you are worried you might miss it, loosely tie a paper bag around the ripening seedhead.

Collect seeds on a dry day, and not first thing in the morning when they may be moist with dew. Paper bags are best for storage, as they won't cause humidity to develop. Store seeds in a cool, dry, frost-free place. And if you're not sure when to sow them, sneak a look at the back of a seed packet.

Collect plenty of seeds and save only those that look undamaged and healthy. To increase the chances of variation, keep a selection of, say, dark and white seeds, or large and small.

Hollyhock
(*Alcea*)

RANDOM HARVEST *above*
For informal plantings where you don't mind what colour pops up, some seeds of cottagey plants like these are definitely worth collecting.

IN THE BAG *above*
Hold an open paper bag beneath the seedhead and tap or shake the stem. Here, the ripe seeds of Jacob's ladder (*Polemonium*) fall readily into the bag.

Case "pings" open to release seeds

HEAD START
Collecting the seeds from *Echinops* (*left*) is easy, but they are then best stored for sowing the following spring. The ripened heads of ornamental alliums (*right*) readily release their seeds when shaken, but still leave you with a very pretty seedhead which you can use in a dried arrangement.

New plants from old

ONE OF GARDENING'S RICHEST REWARDS, for me, is its marvellous sense of continuity – and the fact that you can grow lots of new plants from bits of your old ones has definite economic appeal too! I still get a real thrill every time I see the first signs that a cutting has taken and is starting to grow away on its own roots. Also, while garden centres and nurseries may have a good selection they can't possibly stock everything, and (all too often) the particular variety that you have admired in someone else's garden cannot be found. Ask if you can take cuttings or beg a few offsets of bulbs – most gardeners will be only too flattered that you want to imitate their choice.

When taking any plant material to propagate, always select it from your healthiest, most vigorous-looking plants as they should produce the best results.

Experienced gardeners bend the rules when it comes to timing, but you really do get the best results by waiting for the correct season.

SEPARATING OFFSETS

Most bulbs multiply very obligingly, producing offspring, or "offsets", around the parent bulb. The clump becomes overcrowded and usually benefits from being lifted and divided. It is best to do this when the plants are dormant, although snowdrops are an exception; divide them after flowering.

In the process you can separate off numerous small bulbs, discarding any that look unhealthy, and replant them immediately on freshly prepared ground. They may take a year or two to reach flowering size, so keep them in a less prominent area and feed well until they are large enough to flower.

Parent bulb

Young offsets

Put a label in the ground by your newly planted offsets so that you know what you have planted, and where.

Avoid using offsets from bulbs with foliage that show signs of disease such as streaking.

CUTTINGS

Softwood cuttings are young, succulent shoots, either the tips of new stems, cut about six leaves down (usually in late spring or early summer), or early shoots that spring from the crown of the plant (basal cuttings). Semi-ripe cuttings are taken when growth is starting to turn woody, usually in mid- to late summer, again cutting about six leaves down, except in some shrubbier plants, where you pull off a sideshoot with a tag, or "heel", of bark from the main stem.

TAKING CUTTINGS WITH A HEEL

1 If the cutting requires a heel, carefully pull the shoot you want away from the main stem so that it comes away with the swelling at the joint attached to the base.

2 Always choose healthy, vigorous-looking stems for cuttings. Now that this one has been separated from the plant you can clearly see the heel with a small strip of bark attached.

3 Hold the cutting firmly and use a sharp knife to cut off any excess bark, neatening up the edge of the heel in the process. Plant as soon as possible and do not leave in bright sunlight.

DIVIDING FLESHY ROOTS

Some plants – such as irises and bergenias – have thick, fleshy roots, called rhizomes, close to the soil surface. As the plant forms a spreading clump, the rhizomes in the middle tend to become old and bare. Division allows you to rejuvenate the clump and gain extra plants. Drive a fork in at an angle well away from the clump to minimize injury, lift the rhizomes and shake off excess soil.

1 Split the rhizomes, discard any that look unhealthy and keep those parts that are vigorous. Dusting cut surfaces with sulphur helps to keep them disease-free.

2 Use a sharp knife or scissors to cut back the foliage. This helps to keep the new plant stable in the ground and reduces moisture loss from the foliage.

3 Each rhizome section looks healthy and has enough roots attached to keep it alive until more form. Plant the rhizomes close to the soil surface.

DIVIDING CLUMPS

Most clump-forming herbaceous perennials, especially those that have a wide-spreading root system or lots of basal shoots, are easy to divide, giving you several new, small but reinvigorated plants. This is best done in autumn or early spring. When you lift the plant, take the opportunity to weed the soil around it thoroughly, and fork in some organic matter.

1 After lifting, pull or cut the plant into sections. Divide large or tough clumps by inserting two forks back to back into the clump to prise it apart.

2 Separate each division using a sharp knife, then neaten up cut surfaces. Replant the sections immediately, choosing the healthiest and most vigorous.

Make sure that each section has plenty of thin, fibrous "feeding" roots. Divide plants in a cool, shady spot to keep them in good condition. Once replanted, keep well watered and protected from temperature extremes.

On heavy soils divide plants in spring; on light soils autumn is usually better.

ROOTING CUTTINGS

1 Remove the lowermost leaves to leave about 5cm (2in) of clear stem. Dip the base of the cutting in hormone rooting powder (to stimulate root formation) and tap sharply to shake off excess.

2 Insert the cutting into the compost and firm the compost carefully against its base. Water well with mains water. Keep well watered and supply with bottom heat in a propagator, if needed.

STARTING CUTTINGS OFF
Use a small pot to encourage the roots to grow out to the sides.

Take cuttings early in the day when the plants show no signs of heat stress.

Check the requirements of the cuttings you have taken – some do better in humid conditions, some may need the heat of a propagator. The type of compost they will thrive in also varies.

Water cuttings with mains water. Water from a butt often contains harmful organisms.

Keeping up appearances

ONE OF THE MOST USEFUL JOBS you can do in the garden is to walk around inspecting it regularly. By nipping out a dead flowerhead or new weed here, or making a mental note of overcrowding or some slug damage there, you can keep the garden looking great and stop little jobs piling up to become a weekend slog. Allow plenty of time to admire your handiwork, too, and it'll hardly seem like work at all!

WATERING

An adequate and regular supply of water is essential for most flowers. Water needs will vary depending on the plant, the site, the season and weather conditions, but there are several general rules that are worth observing. Always water gently, taking care to avoid eroding the soil from around the base of the plant. This gives water time to seep through to the roots, reducing run-off. It's best to water in the evening, especially during hot weather, minimizing loss due to evaporation.

When planting, to conserve water, plant in a slight depression or insert a pipe to run from the soil surface to the root ball.

Add water-retaining polymer granules to containers; check the packet for the correct amount.

If the soil is very dry, to reduce run-off, water it briefly to moisten the surface, then water thoroughly shortly afterwards.

MULCHING

A layer of mulch added to the soil surface helps to reduce moisture loss from the soil due to evaporation and helps to deter weeds. I prefer to use natural material that allows water to reach the roots, such as composted bark, chipped bark, cocoa shells or gravel, although black plastic sheeting is a cheaper option. Before mulching, remove weeds and water the soil thoroughly first. Mulch the whole bed or at least each individual plant's root area, leaving a small circle clear around the crown.

Gravel is an effective mulch that can be laid directly on the soil or used to camouflage a layer of plastic sheeting. It will require little or no maintenance.

FEEDING

Although most garden soils contain a good range of plant nutrients, it is worth adding some fertilizer to ensure that plants receive plenty of everything they need to flower well. There are many different types, organic and artificial, which come in the form of liquids, powders, granules, or controlled-release pellets or sticks. Some contain a broad spectrum of nutrients and may be described as "general", or "complete"; others are more restricted in content and serve a specific purpose.

Wear gloves when handling powdered fertilizer and avoid sprinkling it on the plant.

Always check the product label for the N:P:K ratio — the ratio of nitrogen to phosphorus to potassium — and other information as to what the fertilizer is best used for.

Check timing and quantities before you apply; fertilizer applied in the wrong season or amount may be of little benefit.

DEADHEADING

Removing faded flowerheads makes a difference to a plant's performance. Unless those shrivelled, unattractive brown flowers are removed promptly, the plant usually starts to produce a seedhead, fruit or pod. This means that both the number of flowers produced and the length of the flowering period start to decrease. There is also a risk that fungi such as grey mould will invade the dead flower and possibly kill the plant. To be most effective, deadhead regularly and as soon as the flowers have faded.

SHORT-STEMMED FLOWERS
Plants that produce lots of flowers in quick succession like these petunias need very frequent deadheading. As each individual flower stem is extremely short, just pinch off the faded blooms.

PROVIDING SUPPORT

Supports help to keep plants compact when they might otherwise tend to flop, and ensure that unwieldy flower stems remain straight and unbroken. Always get stakes or other plant supports in position as early as possible so that the plant develops naturally around them.

READY-MADE SUPPORT
Purpose-made, plastic-coated or galvanized wire supports have individual sections that you link together to create a support of the precise size and shape you need – ideal for floppy leaves, and soon hidden as plants grow.

SINGLE CANE
Tall, heavy, individual flower stems – here of a delphinium – often need support. Insert a cane close to the crown and tie the flower stem to it at intervals as it develops. To prevent eye injury, top with a cane guard.

TWIGGY STICKS
A subtle support system is easy to construct using twiggy sticks driven into the soil around the crown of the plant. Use them for plants with delicate stems or for patio container plants for an elegant effect.

CANES AND TWINE
Vigorously growing plants may need sturdier support to prevent flopping, especially in windy sites. Drive several canes into the soil around the main bulk of the plant, then tie garden twine so that it links the canes together.

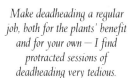

LONG-STEMMED FLOWERS
For most plants that have long, bare flower stems, such as this rudbeckia, it is best to cut the entire flower stem, complete with the faded bloom, down to its point of origin at a main stem.

FLOWER HEADS AND SPIKES
Use secateurs or sharp scissors to remove just the faded flowerheads from flower stems that carry leaves, which are useful to the plant; there may also be more flower buds lower down.

TRIMMING OVER
With some plants such as lavender you can deadhead all at once, and tidy up the plant too, by giving it a quick "haircut" with shears. This also helps to encourage dense, bushy growth.

Make deadheading a regular job, both for the plants' benefit and for your own – I find protracted sessions of deadheading very tedious.

If you want to save some seed, remove all but a few developing seedheads and you should still get plenty of flowers.

Periods of heavy summer rain often damage petals, so you may find there is plenty of deadheading to do afterwards.

Secrets of success

HOWEVER CAREFULLY YOU CHOOSE your plants and then nurture them, both pests and diseases and extremes of weather are likely to cause problems at some stage. Although such problems may be disheartening they are rarely very serious, and the plant can usually be restored to good health without your having to expend a great deal of effort. If there's no option but to lose a plant, don't be despondent – as the wisest gardeners say, a dead plant isn't a failure but a wonderful new planting opportunity!

Make a note of when you carry out seasonal tasks so that you will remember to do them at the correct time next year. For example, if late frosts occur, mark the date in your garden diary so you don't remove winter protection too early.

YOUR FRIENDS IN THE GARDEN

Not all wildlife visitors to your garden are pests. Many of them are very beneficial, and, provided you can supply them with at least some of their habitat needs, they will reward you with cost-free, natural pest control. Any water feature – especially a pond – acts like a magnet, enticing many potentially useful animals, which use the water for drinking, grooming or breeding. Growing a wide range of plants helps, too, particularly if you can include some that have plenty of readily accessible nectar (see Flowers for Bees and Butterflies, pp.138–9). Being too tidy and clearing up all debris and dead plant material at the end of the season may discourage garden friends. You may be removing their breeding or overwintering places, so always try to leave a few hideaways.

Ladybird feeding on aphids

Use pesticides only when absolutely necessary. Choose products that specifically target the problem, so minimizing damage to other creatures.

Plenty of insects are either harmless or beneficial. Relatively few are pests, so always identify them before you spray or squash!

DISEASE AND PEST PATROL

Keeping your eyes open as you go round the garden is often all it takes to keep many pests and diseases in check. Take a container with you and collect up and dispose of the culprits or the affected leaves. By taking such simple measures it may be possible to stop potentially serious problems in their tracks. If you don't want to use chemicals at all, you may need to dispose of badly infested plants. After a few seasons you will get to know the "high-risk" plants in your garden and perhaps consider alternatives.

POWDERY MILDEW
If this greyish-white fungal layer appears (often in dry spells), pick off affected leaves or other plant parts. Keep plants well watered at the roots, but avoid wetting the foliage. Consider spraying with a suitable fungicide.

GREY MOULD (BOTRYTIS)
Avoid injuring plants and remove dead or damaged areas promptly, before they're attacked by this fuzzy grey fungal growth. Poor air circulation encourages it, so separate crowded plants. Consider spraying with a fungicide.

APHIDS
Greenfly and blackfly feed by sucking plant sap, often causing distortion and poor growth, and may spread viruses too. Spray with a suitable insecticide, preferably one containing the aphid-specific pirimicarb.

EXTREMES OF TEMPERATURE

Plants may need protecting against weather extremes, especially when they are newly planted and not yet properly established. In frost-prone climates, protection may enable you to keep plants over winter that otherwise would not survive. The protection need not be expensive or too time-consuming to provide, and the benefits are usually well worth any effort involved.

Never buy and plant out summer bedding too early, however tempting it may look in the garden centre.

Plants sold as summer bedding aren't meant to live through winter. Even if a few scruffy specimens miraculously survive, they're better replaced with strong young plants.

SUMMER PROTECTION
Some plants, particularly clematis, may enjoy a fairly sunny fence or wall over which to scramble, but at the same time need to have their roots kept cool if they are to thrive. Placing old roof tiles, slates or pebbles around the base solves the problem, keeping the soil shaded and retaining moisture. They have the added bonus that they can be arranged to look decorative, too.

WINTER PROTECTION
Plants in containers are particularly prone to damage by frosts because they are grown above ground. Soil moisture may also be unavailable. Wrapping the whole container securely in hessian affords the plant several degrees of protection. Old curtains, bubblewrap polythene or similar material will work just as efficiently, although as far as appearance goes the effect will be less attractive.

MULCHING FOR WARMTH
Covering half-hardy or not fully hardy perennials with a deep mulch may often be sufficient to allow them to survive all but the coldest weather. It may mean you do not need to lift the plants each autumn, and is especially useful for plants that are young or recently planted, which are often more susceptible. Choose dry, loose materials such as chipped bark, as winter wet is often just as damaging as cold.

CATERPILLARS
Most caterpillars feed in groups on leaves, leaving holes. They usually feed after dusk, so check plants at this time. Pick off by hand if possible, or you can spray affected plants with a suitable insecticide or biological control.

EARWIGS
Often feeding at night and eating extensive holes in flower buds, petals and young leaves, these pests often hide in amongst the plants during the day. Set earwig traps or consider spraying with a suitable insecticide.

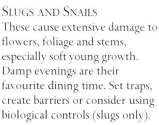

SLUGS AND SNAILS
These cause extensive damage to flowers, foliage and stems, especially soft young growth. Damp evenings are their favourite dining time. Set traps, create barriers or consider using biological controls (slugs only).

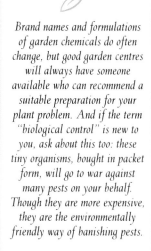

Brand names and formulations of garden chemicals do often change, but good garden centres will always have someone available who can recommend a suitable preparation for your plant problem. And if the term "biological control" is new to you, ask about this too: these tiny organisms, bought in packet form, will go to war against many pests on your behalf. Though they are more expensive, they are the environmentally friendly way of banishing pests.

FAVOURITE FLOWERS

Spikes & spires

HOW FLAT THE FLOWER GARDEN WOULD BE WITHOUT SPIKES AND SPIRES. FROM THE COOL, SECRETIVE BEAUTY OF FOXGLOVES TO MASSED RANKS OF COLOURFUL SALVIAS, THESE PLANTS HAVE undeniable poise and impact. But, despite their stature and presence, few of them could be accused of being stand-offish – many owe their popularity to the cottage gardeners of old, and they are just as happy in a more relaxed, rustic planting as in a formal border. On most the flowers open gradually over a long period, and this, combined with their striking, often pencil-thin outlines and their tremendous range of colours and heights, makes spikes and spires invaluable in any garden, large or small. Most make ideal candidates for the back or middle of a border, but a clump of tall spires on its own also makes a fantastic focal point.

"Who can resist these elegant yet sturdy spires as they stand, straight-backed, like soldiers on parade?"

DELPHINIUMS, PAGES 32–3

Left FOXGLOVES (PP.42–3), COOL AND ELEGANT IN A WOODLAND SETTING

Delphiniums *DELPHINIUM*

WHO CAN RESIST THESE elegant yet sturdy spires as they stand, straight-backed, like soldiers on parade? Despite this air of formality, delphiniums are surprisingly versatile, and they are as much at home in a cottage-style garden as in a traditional herbaceous border. Even when they are not in flower, their lush, deeply cut foliage forms an attractive mound, provided you can keep it free from the ravages of slugs!

◄ FLOWER SPIKE 25cm (10in) long

CREAM ON TOP *above*
'Sungleam' has creamy-white flower spikes with yellow centres, mixing well with other colours.

WHITER THAN WHITE *left*
The flowers of 'Clear Spring' are really packed together along its stems, creating impressive, pure white towers in summer.

BROWN-EYED GIRL
The semi-double, delicate pink, brown-eyed flower spikes of 'Rosemary Brock' look lovely planted with the lilac-mauve delphinium 'Conspicuous'.

ROYAL FLUSH
The small, delicate flowers of 'Atlantis', a Belladonna Group perennial, are a truly regal purple, and their fine foliage matches their elegant demeanour.

GROWING DELPHINIUMS

PLANT PROFILE

Hardy perennials, though the Pacific Hybrids – 'Black Knight', 'King Arthur', and so on – are quite short-lived.

• SIZE 90–180cm (3–6ft).

• FLOWER COLOURS Red, blue, purple, lilac, pink, white.

• FLOWERING Early to mid-summer.

• SITE Best in reasonably well-drained, rich soil, in full sun, sheltered from strong winds.

Sowing seeds Seed can be sown directly into the soil in spring. The seeds do not last long and are best sown as soon as possible after collection or after the packet has been opened. To keep seed over winter, store at 2–5°C (36–41°F) until you can sow them.

Dividing Divide established plants in spring, or take basal cuttings in spring.

Flower care As soon as the flower spike has faded, cut back to a vigorous, healthy leaf. This not only tidies up the plant, but often encourages a second, later flush of flowers.

For cutting Delphiniums make excellent cut flowers. Cut just as the first buds start to open.

My favourites 'Blue Bird'; 'Blue Dawn'; 'Blue Fountains'; 'Blue Nile'; 'Bruce'; 'Butterball'; *Delphinium cardinale*; 'Centurion Sky Blue'; 'Chelsea Star'; 'Dwarf Snow White'; *D. grandiflorum, D. g.* 'Blue Butterfly'; 'Strawberry Fair'; the Pacific Hybrids 'Astolat', 'Black Knight', 'Cameliard', 'Galahad', 'Guinevere' and 'King Arthur'.

BLUE CLASSIC *right*
For a really traditional delphinium, this fantastic form of 'Clear Spring' is hard to beat. Its purple-blue flowers each have a contrasting ruffled white centre and are closely packed on sturdy stems.

◀ FLOWER SPIKE 40cm (16in) long

CROWNING GLORY

The towering spikes of tall delphiniums are ideal for the back of the flower border; plant them in groups for maximum impact. Place medium to small varieties closer to the front, where they will add stature without obscuring the view through to plants behind.

Where possible, plant delphiniums out of prevailing winds. Stake flower spikes with stout canes early in the season and with care, avoiding injury to the base of the plant. Pea sticks are fine for dwarf varieties.

Penstemons *PENSTEMON*

FORMING CLUMPS OF TALL, graceful flower stems year after year, penstemons are excellent value. They are easy to look after, they don't need staking or pruning, and they will flower throughout the summer and into mid-autumn, sometimes even later if they escape early frosts, helping to bring colour at a time when many border plants are past their best. Penstemons need a well-drained soil with plenty of sun, a regular supply of moisture during the growing season, and protection from winter cold (many are not fully hardy).

◄ FLOWER
SPIKE
20cm (8in)
long

BOUNTIFUL LADY
Although smaller than some other varieties, the purplish-pink flowers of 'Catherine de la Mare' are produced in great profusion.

RED ALERT
The brilliant red flowers of 'Garnet' shine out in any border like the semi-precious gems after which they are named.

SOLO STAR
With its large, cerise-red flowers and clearly defined white throat, 'Maurice Gibbs' makes an impact even when grown singly.

NOBLE PURPLE *above*
The purply-red flowers of 'Countess of Dalkeith', each with a distinctive white throat, have considerable poise and elegance.

BLAZE OF GLORY *right*
When grown amongst other late summer and early autumn flowers, 'Garnet' makes a dazzling and uninhibited trail of glowing red. As with all penstemons, regular deadheading will help to prolong the flowering period.

For really small spaces, consider growing alpine penstemons, which are suited to troughs or a rock garden.

Under most conditions, penstemons retain their foliage over the winter. However, don't worry if occasionally the foliage dies off. Clear it away and watch for regrowth in the following spring.

GROWING PENSTEMONS

PLANT PROFILE

Hardiness varies, so it is best to treat most of them as slightly tender perennials.

- SIZE Most 60–90cm (2–3ft).
- FLOWER COLOURS Red, purple, lilac, pink, white, cream.
- FLOWERING From mid-summer through to mid-autumn.
- SITE Well-drained soil, in plenty of sun.

Cuttings None of the named varieties can be raised from seed, so buy new plants or take cuttings in late summer and overwinter them in a frost-free cold frame or greenhouse. Plant out in late spring.

Soil A well-drained soil is essential. If yours is heavy, dig in lots of grit and garden compost to improve drainage and add extra grit to the planting hole. Mulching helps conserve moisture around roots in summer.

Protection Each winter, mulch individual plants with a deep layer of chipped bark, held in place with a piece of chicken wire. In very cold areas or if a particularly severe winter is forecast, either bring plants into a frost-free cold frame or greenhouse, or take cuttings in case the plant does not survive.

My favourites 'Alice Hindley', 'Apple Blossom', *Penstemon barbatus*, 'Burgundy', 'Catherine de la Mare', 'Chester Scarlet', 'Countess of Dalkeith', *P. digitalis* 'Albus', 'Firebird', 'Garnet', 'Maurice Gibbs', 'Osprey', 'Port Wine', 'Rubicundus', 'Sour Grapes', 'Stapleford Gem', 'White Bedder'.

TIMELESS ELEGANCE *right*
The classic, elegant flowers of 'Stapleford Gem' are closely packed up the stems in subtle shades of purple and pink. As with all other penstemons, ensure that the roots are kept moist or the number of flower spikes and the length of the flowering period will be reduced.

Lupins *LUPINUS*

ALTHOUGH LUPINS ARE classic cottage-garden flowers, I find that they look just as at ease in a formal border as they do in a back yard or informal planting. Above luxurious-looking mounds of pale green, star-like leaves, the dense flowerheads form long-lasting spires of colour for much of the summer. Although these hardy perennials will perform in most conditions, they prefer, if possible, a slightly acid soil. Lupins will attract plenty of bees into your garden, especially on a warm, sunny day.

RAINBOW'S END *above*
Available in a wide range of colours, the Russell Hybrids reliably produce cheerful hordes of densely packed flower spikes throughout the summer.

SOLID COLOUR
Choosing and grouping single-colour lupins such as 'Chandelier' allows you to create strong blocks of colour in a more coordinated border.

SPICE OF LIFE
Be bold and treat yourself to some of the more brightly coloured lupins that are now available. Here, 'The Page', one of my passions, brings red-hot hues into your garden.

◄ FLOWER SPIKE
25cm (10in)
long

SMALL IS BEAUTIFUL *left*
In smaller gardens or towards the front of the border, shorter varieties such as this gorgeous, richly coloured dwarf Minarette are especially useful.

MIX AND MATCH
Bicoloured flowers, like
this pink and yellow
Minarette, fascinate
amateur lupin
breeders and
exhibition
growers.

PERFECT HARMONY *above*
Lupins have no great reputation for subtlety, but
even the brashest colours can work in mixed
plantings. Here, the pinkish-red and white
flowers of 'The Chatelaine' are easy on the eye
among irises, ornamental alliums and chives.

GROWING LUPINS

PLANT PROFILE
Fully hardy to half-hardy
annuals and perennials.
- SIZE Most 75–105cm
(30–42in).
- FLOWER COLOURS Red,
orange, yellow, blue, purple,
lilac, pink, white, cream; many
bicolours.
- FLOWERING Early summer
to early autumn.
- SITE Well-drained, neutral to
acid soil, in sun or part shade.

Sowing seeds Sow seeds of
annuals in open ground in spring.
Perennials grown from seed need to
spend their first year under glass.

Soil Improve drainage of heavy soil
by adding plenty of grit before
planting, or choose a sloping site
where drainage will be better. Do
not overfeed.

Growing tip Remove the flower
spike in the plant's first year; this
will greatly increase vigour.

My favourites 'Chandelier',
'Dwarf Lulu', Minarette Group,
Gallery Series, 'Kayleigh Ann
Savage', 'My Castle', 'Noble Maiden',
'Pope John Paul', Russell
Hybrids, ' The Chatelaine',
'The Governor',
'The Page'.

*To save your own seed, cut off
all bar the lowest few whorls of
faded flowers. Leaving the
whole spike to develop seed
will seriously weaken the
plant, and the resultant seeds
will be much smaller.*

*Named varieties do not come
true from seed, so if you collect
your own, be prepared for
plenty of variation.*

◀ FLOWER SPIKE
25cm (10in)
long

Red-hot pokers *KNIPHOFIA*

I FIND RED-HOT POKERS more fascinating than beautiful, but there's no disputing that their proud, flame-coloured flower spikes are absolute show-stoppers in a summer border. Sometimes also referred to as torch lilies, these perennials are surprisingly easy to grow in a sheltered spot in sun or part shade, and there are many different varieties to choose from, in numerous shades of red, orange, yellow, cream and bronze.

COOL CUSTOMER
The diminutive 'Little Maid' belies *Kniphofia*'s common name, with cool, milky-yellow flowers on a dainty stem.

MORNING GLORY
For summertime echoes of a tequila sunrise cocktail, 'Bees' Sunset' is flushed orange to yellow down its flower stem.

WHITE HEAT
It may be called 'Strawberries and Cream', but to me this red-hot poker looks as if it has reached white-hot at the base!

GROWING RED-HOT POKERS

PLANT PROFILE

Hardy perennials; they need a sheltered spot in regions with cold winters.

- SIZE 60–150cm (2–5ft).
- FLOWER COLOURS Red, orange, yellow, cream, bronze.
- FLOWERING The majority flower in mid-summer.
- SITE Free-draining soil is especially important in winter. They prefer full sun, but will do well in part shade.

Soil Red-hot pokers really do need a well-drained soil. Don't let these otherwise easy plants suffer from winter wet or they will simply rot and die off.

Choosing plants By checking the flowering periods carefully before you buy you can, if you wish, have varieties coming into flower from one end of summer to the other.

Sowing seeds Sow seed of species and mixed varieties in autumn or spring. Grow seedlings on and transplant into flowering positions one year later. Seed-raised plants will need to be kept under glass until they are at least one year old. The more flamboyant red-hot pokers are the named varieties, which do not come true from seed.

Planting Incorporate grit in the planting hole and surrounding area if your soil is on the heavy side; this will decrease the likelihood of the plant suffering from damp in winter.

Dividing Divide established plants carefully in either autumn or spring. Unlike many other rhizomatous-rooted plants, red-hot pokers are not inclined to spread extensively and usually keep themselves in neat clumps.

Protection A mulch of chipped bark or other free-draining material is advisable to ensure that new plants survive their first couple of winters unscathed. Winter wet is more likely to prove fatal than low temperatures. In particularly cold areas an annual mulch in autumn helps to protect the crown in winter.

My favourites 'Alcazar', 'Bees' Sunset', *Kniphofia caulescens*, 'Cobra', 'Ice Queen', 'Little Maid', 'Samuel's Sensation', 'Toffee Nosed'.

GARDEN SIZZLERS
The warm, relaxing pinks and purples of this border, which include clematis, tamarisk, verbenas and salvias, are given a dramatic lift by the presence of a large clump of red-hot pokers.

FLOWER SPIKE ▷
22cm (8½in)
long

DYING EMBERS
As summer ends, red-hot pokers are slowly quenched, from bottom to top. Dying flowers are not normally eye-catching, but in *Kniphofia linearifolia* the faded brown tones in well with the still-vibrant red and orange.

If, despite your efforts, your red-hot pokers do not thrive, flower well or even survive and you suspect that your soil is too damp for them in winter, try replanting them on slight mounds to ensure that excess water drains away from around the base of the plants. You could also add garden grit to the soil to improve drainage further. Water well in dry spells in the next summer.

TOWERING INFERNO
One of the classic red-hot pokers is 'Alcazar'. Its elongated, finger-like flowers bring a glowing warmth wherever you plant it.

Long stamens of bright yellow hang gracefully from open flowers

Verbascums *VERBASCUM*

THESE TALL, flower-decked columns are perfect for the middle or back of the border or in island beds. Verbascums also look lovely if allowed to self-seed and naturalize around the edge of a tree's canopy or in a wild garden, provided it is a reasonably sunny site. As well as their beautiful flower spikes, which attract crowds of bees, many varieties have sumptuous, silvery, furry rosettes of foliage. As long as these perennials get lots of sunshine and, if possible, a poor, well-drained alkaline soil (these plants definitely do not like being fed too well), they will reward you with a bold display throughout the summer and often well into autumn.

OLYMPIAN HEIGHTS
One of the tallest and most imposing of the verbascums, *Verbascum olympicum* is often extensively branched towards the base of the flower spike, forming a fat plume.

DELICATE WHITES
Verbascum chaixii 'Album' bears tall spikes of tiny white flowers with contrasting mauve centres, useful for lightening borders of many colours. The leaves are semi-evergreen.

PRETTY AS A PICTURE
The subtly coloured flowers of *Verbascum chaixii* 'Gainsborough' remind me of primroses in spring. They produce a long-lasting display over a rosette of semi-evergreen foliage.

PRIMA DONNA
Throughout the summer, *Verbascum chaixii* 'Cotswold Queen' reigns supreme, producing unbranched spikes of bright yellow flowers with purple-brown centres.

GROWING VERBASCUMS

PLANT PROFILE

Biennials, perennials, a few annuals; most are hardy. Less hardy varieties need winter protection.

• SIZE 30–150cm (1–5ft); most are 90–120cm (3–4ft) tall.

• FLOWER COLOURS Yellow, purple, lilac, pink, white, brown.

• FLOWERING Throughout summer and into autumn.

• SITE Ideally, a very poor and free-draining soil, in full sun.

Raising plants Some verbascums can be raised from seed, but root cuttings are the best method for propagating named varieties. Take root cuttings, about 7.5cm (3in) long, in early spring. Root them in a mixture of half peat and half sand in a cold frame. Once the young plants have three or four leaves, pot them individually, then plant out in the flower bed in autumn. You can divide mature perennial varieties in spring.

Protection The less hardy varieties 'Golden Wings' and 'Letitia' and the species *Verbascum dumulosum* need a sheltered site and good drainage. If in doubt as to whether these can be provided, cover plants during winter to protect them from cold and damp.

My favourites *Verbascum chaixii* 'Album', *V. c.* 'Cotswold Beauty', *V. c.* 'Gainsborough', *V. c.* 'Pink Domino'; *V. dumulosum* (hardy only in a sheltered spot); 'Helen Johnson'.

In the right conditions, most verbascums self-seed readily. They may not be true to type, but are well worth keeping.

A SECOND GLANCE, *right*
'Helen Johnson' is one of the few "trendy" plants I've allowed myself to fall in love with, although I admit the pinkish-brown flowers are an acquired taste.

GREY EMINENCE *above*
The enormous, woolly, grey-leaved verbascums such as *Verbascum bombyciferum*, *V. chaixii* (nettle-leaved mullein) and *V. olympicum* form dramatic, architectural towers of foliage which add a spectacular focal point to the garden long before the first flower opens.

All surfaces are covered in a dense grey down

FLOWER SPIKE ▶
25cm (10in) long

Foxgloves *DIGITALIS*

WHY SETTLE FOR a flat expanse of ground cover under trees and large shrubs, when you can accentuate vertical shafts of dappled sunlight with the palely glimmering, coolly elegant spires of foxgloves? Most bear their first and finest flowers in their second year, after which they are best replaced. However, foxgloves are formidable self-seeders and, provided you are happy with a rather unpredictable mixture of flower shades in their offspring, will perpetuate themselves almost indefinitely.

SOLO PERFORMANCE
For a single-colour effect the warm shades of 'Sutton's Apricot' are particularly hard to resist. The colour fades as flowers open.

AN EASY FIT
The unassuming, delicate slipper-like flowers of *Digitalis grandiflora* are especially well suited to a wild or natural garden.

If you want to save seed from white foxgloves, grow the parent plants as far away as possible from foxgloves in other colours for the best chance of white-flowered seedlings. Alternatively, buy fresh seed every year.

All parts of the foxglove are dangerous if eaten, and contact with the foliage can irritate some skins, so keep them away from small children playing in the garden.

◄ FLOWER SPIKE
60–75cm
(24–30in) long

FAST AND FOXY *above*
The Foxy hybrids of *Digitalis purpurea* are hardy enough to be sown outdoors in early spring, and will usually be in flower by midsummer of the same year.

WOODLAND IDYLL *right*
Although they are equally at home in a sunny border, the dream-like quality of foxgloves really comes through under the boughs of a spreading tree.

GROWING FOXGLOVES

PLANT PROFILE

Hardy biennials and perennials.

- SIZE 45–150cm (18–60in).
- FLOWER COLOURS Yellow, purple, lilac, pink, white, cream, brown.
- FLOWERING Early summer to early autumn.
- SITE Any soil will do, provided it is not too wet or too dry, in full sun or any but heavy shade.

Sowing seeds Sow direct outside in late spring or early summer for flowers in the following year.

Self-seeding As soon as self-sown seedlings beneath a plant are about 10cm (4in) tall they can be moved, if desired. Take a good trowelful of soil with the roots and keep very well watered after transplanting. Because foxgloves cross-pollinate very readily, offspring rarely look the same as the parent plants.

Siting Planted in a shady spot, a foxglove grows much taller than if planted in sun, so bear this in mind when planning.

Support Provided they are not over-fed nor grown in an exposed site, staking should not be necessary.

Flower care If faded flower spikes are removed promptly, a new flush of flower spikes may develop, sometimes several months later.

My favourites *Digitalis ferruginea; D. grandiflora; D. laevigata* subsp. *graeca; D. lanata; D. lutea; D. × mertonensis; D. purpurea, D. p.* f. *albiflora, D. p.* 'Sutton's Apricot' (sometimes called 'Apricot Beauty', or even just 'Apricot'), *D. p.* Excelsior Group, *D. p.* Foxy Group; *D. viridiflora.*

A CUT ABOVE *right*
The small hybrid foxglove
Digitalis × mertonensis is especially good as a cut flower; like all other foxgloves, it is guaranteed to attract hosts of bees to your garden.

Hollyhocks *ALCEA ROSEA*

ALTHOUGH NINETEENTH-CENTURY artists often depicted hollyhocks standing bolt upright in tidy, "chocolate-box" cottage gardens, I must admit I like to leave mine unstaked in the more informal areas of my garden to flop as they will. For a more dramatic effect, they look striking lined up in a row against a wall, or neatly staked around the edges of a vegetable plot. These hardy biennials or perennials thrive in a heavy soil in full sun or in a slightly shaded position, but aren't too fussy — I've even seen a runaway seedling growing from a crack in tarmac.

MIXED BLESSINGS *left*
Sow a packet of Single Mix seed and you are guaranteed long-lasting, eye-catching flowers in tempting shades of purple, pink, white, cream and yellow.

◀ FLOWER SIZE
5−10cm (2−4in) across

Flowers open in succession from the base of the spire to the tip

DOUBLE TAKE
With flowers just like paper pompons, 'Chater's Double' and other double-flowered forms have a much blowsier style than the single form.

BLACK BEAUTY
Why bother searching for a black tulip when you can so easily have spikes of the gorgeous, silky-smooth, purple-black flowers of hollyhock 'Nigra'?

GROWING HOLLYHOCKS

PLANT PROFILE

Most are hardy perennials or biennials. Give them a winter mulch in cold areas.

• SIZE 1.2–2.4m (4–8ft).

• FLOWER COLOURS Red, yellow, purple, lilac, pink, white, cream.

• FLOWERING Summer, often into early autumn.

• SITE Heavy soil in full sun or part shade, preferably in a sheltered spot.

Planting Add general fertilizer to the soil before planting and feed throughout the summer. An annual autumn mulch of compost or well-rotted horse manure is beneficial.

Sowing seeds Sow seeds direct in summer or spring the year before the flowering plants are desired. If you are able to provide heat (13°C/55°F), you can sow seeds under glass in late winter. Harden them off and plant out in mid-spring for flowers that summer.

Plant problems Hollyhocks are very prone to a fungal rust disease that can devastate their foliage and seriously weaken the plants. Raising your own plants will ensure that they start out rust-free. Spray young and mature plants regularly with a suitable fungicide.

My favourites 'Chater's Double', in apricot or mixed; 'Majorette'; 'Nigra'; Single Mix.

Hollyhock seeds are easy to collect and although they are unlikely to come true, you will still have beautiful flowers.

Single Mix can flower along at least 90cm (3ft) of the stem

◄ FLOWER SIZE 7.5cm (3in) across

SITTING PRETTY
Hollyhocks look most at home in the cottage garden. Here, next to the branches of a deep purple buddleja, they make a striking wall of colour.

OPEN SEASON *right*
Behind each of the first flowers to open on a hollyhock spire is another plump green pudding of a flower bud waiting its turn – no wonder their display is so long-lasting.

Veronicas *VERONICA*

THE PIERCING BLUE OF classic veronicas – sometimes known as speedwells – is a refreshing sight in any sunny border, and lasts from mid-spring through to early summer. Less widely grown but equally easy to look after are the pink and white forms, which, like the blue veronicas, have a distinct central "eye" to each flower. Most are grown in borders, but some of the smaller varieties are best suited to a rock garden. Once established, veronicas will produce a bold block of colour, though on close inspection each plant is delicate and fragile to look at. They are simple to grow as long as they have plenty of sun and well-drained soil. Bees and butterflies find them irresistible.

OUT OF THE BLUE *right*
One of the taller-growing forms, *Veronica spicata* produces a carpet of bright blue flower spikes set against attractive grey-green foliage.

Tiny individual flowers

GROWING VERONICAS

PLANT PROFILE

Hardy perennials; varieties damaged by winter wet should be brought into a greenhouse.

• SIZE 7.5–50cm (3–20in), but *Veronica virginica* 'Rosea' reaches a towering 1.8m (6ft).

• FLOWER COLOURS Blue, pink, white.

• FLOWERING From mid-spring to early summer.

• SITE Well-drained, poor soil in full sun or slight shade, sheltered from cold winds.

Planting Before planting on a very light or sandy soil, check that it contains a reasonable amount of organic matter. If not, incorporate leaf mould or well-rotted garden compost before planting.

Dividing Divide established clumps in spring or autumn. Dividing every three years helps to keep plants in good condition.

Cuttings Some species are too brittle to divide successfully. Take semi-ripe cuttings in mid-summer and root in a cold frame.

Sowing seeds Only the species can be raised from seed. Sow in early spring in a heated propagator, harden off and put plants into their permanent positions in autumn.

Pruning Remove faded flowers or lightly trim the whole plant when flowering is over. This helps to keep plants compact and encourages better flowering the following year.

Protection *Veronica bombycina* is damaged by cold and wet conditions over winter, so is best avoided unless you have a suitable greenhouse.

Support Plants grown in part shade or exposed positions may need to be given some support. Twiggy branches are best – thick canes will jar among delicate stems.

My favourites *Veronica longifolia*; *V. peduncularis* 'Georgia Blue'; *V. prostrata*, *V. p.* 'Mrs Holt', *V. p.* 'Rosea'; 'Shirley Blue', *V. spicata*; *V. virginica* (sometimes known as *Veronicastrum virginicum*). For very dry conditions, try *V. gentianoides*.

46

COLOUR CONTRAST *above*
The yellow-green foliage of the low-growing *Veronica prostrata* 'Trehane' provides a strong background for the spikes of blue flowers.

Tubular flowers with protruding stamens

FLOWER SPIKE ▶
30cm (12in)
long

Flowers open in succession towards the tip

LOFTY ELEGANCE
One of the taller veronicas, *Veronica virginica* 'Rosea' is topped with slender spikes of delicate pale pink flowers.

LILAC HAZE
The pretty, lilac-blue spikes of *Veronica longifolia* remind me of a miniature version of buddleja, and appear from late summer to early autumn.

FLAT OUT
This mat-forming *Veronica spicata* 'Rotfuchs' only grows to about 30cm (12in) high, but seems larger than life when it breaks out into masses of zingy pink flowers.

In moist ground, grow Veronica beccabunga, which thrives in boggy conditions.

The low-growing V. cinerea is ideal as ground cover. Each plant forms a mat of woody stems 30cm (12in) in diameter.

V. peduncularis forms a mat of bright blue flowers, ideal for growing in between paving.

THINK PINK
With its elegant whorls of languid leaves and its very slim, tapering flowerheads, this pale pink *Veronica virginica* is a real gem for mid-summer to early autumn, when pale pastel colours are rare.

Bold & beautiful

IN FLORAL SOCIAL CIRCLES THEY MAY BE INSUFFERABLE, BUT I LOVE HAVING A FEW REAL SHOW-OFFS IN THE GARDEN. ALL FLOWERS ARE LOVELY, TO BE SURE, BUT THE ONES I'VE CHOSEN here really flaunt their attributes — these are no shrinking violets! All but one of my choices are classic beauties, from statuesque lilies to positively Rubenesque peonies. Some — for example, sweet peas — advertise their voluptuous charms still further with heady perfume, too. Euphorbias might be considered to be imposters in the camp, for their showy "flowers" are in reality conspicuous, brightly coloured leafy bracts, and the tiny and very modest flower in the centre of each often goes unnoticed. Nevertheless, I make no apology for including these truly unusual plants; I find their shape and colour both beautiful and utterly fascinating.

> *"Although their exquisitely silky blooms don't last long, I couldn't bear to miss my annual brief romance with peonies."*
>
> PEONIES, PAGES 54—5

Left IRISES (PP.60—1), AMONG THE MOST STRIKING AND ELEGANT PLANTS IN THE BORDER

Alliums *ALLIUM*

IT'S HARD TO BELIEVE that these close relatives of the humble onion can be so striking. Onions going to seed have flowers that are a lovely shape but are a rather dull and dirty cream; paint them in bright colour, and their exquisite form shouts for attention. Grow these hardy perennials to create tall exclamation marks in a border, or use dwarf varieties to make a carpet of colour throughout the summer. I like to grow alliums in weathered terracotta pots, although wherever I put them I still expect to see a row of cabbages nearby, too!

Pompons are made up of star-shaped flowers

CELESTIAL BLUE
Clusters of powder-blue star-shaped flowers densely grouped together give *Allium caeruleum* a soft, dreamy look.

HOT PINK
Commonly known as the nodding onion, *Allium cernuum* has deep pink, bell-like flowers on exaggerated arching stems.

STAR TURN *right*
This dazzling sphere of colour is *Allium aflatunense* 'Purpureum', with tightly packed, star-shaped flowers of rich pink tinged with purple.

WHITE ON WHITE *above*
When in flower, *Allium stipitatum* 'Album' creates a wonderful show of white and cream pompons. The faded flowerheads left in the border look handsome sparkling in a hoar frost – or bring them indoors to use in dried flower arrangements.

PURPLE DRIFT *left*
This haphazard planting of the purplish-pink *Allium aflatunense* reminds me of brightly coloured hats in a bustling crowd. Close planting with Jacob's ladder (*Polemonium*) in purple and white, herbaceous geraniums and the pinkish-white flowerheads of London pride (*Saxifraga × urbium*) add to the informal air of this border.

Sturdy stems make alliums particularly good for cutting

GROWING ALLIUMS

PLANT PROFILE

Bulbs that flower every year: some alliums benefit from protection during hard frosts.

- SIZE 30–120cm (12–48in).
- FLOWER COLOURS Yellow, blue, purple, lilac, pink, white.
- FLOWERING Throughout the summer and into autumn.
- SITE Fertile, well-drained soil in full sun is essential; incorporate grit on planting to improve drainage.

Planting Plant bulbs 5–10cm (2–4in) deep in mid- to late autumn.

Dividing Congested clumps can be divided in autumn or spring.

Support Tall plants may need staking in exposed gardens.

Plant care Unless you are saving them for drying, remove the flowerheads as soon as they have faded. The stems and foliage should be left on the plant until the autumn, when they can be removed.

My favourites *Allium aflatunense, A. caeruleum, A. cernuum, A. flavum, A. giganteum, A. karataviense, A. neapolitanum, A. oreophilum* (syn. *A. ostrowskianum), A. sphaerocephalon, A. unifolium.* For naturalizing under shrubs, *Allium moly* and *A. triquetrum* are both good. *A. cristophii* has flowerheads up to 20cm (8in) in diameter, and is among the best for winter decoration.

For scent, grow Allium triquetrum, whose white and green striped flowers appear in mid-spring. It can be very invasive; for something less aggressive, choose A. cowanii, with white flowers in mid- to late spring.

Dried allium seedheads make superb winter additions to flower arrangements. As the flowers fade, cut the stems using sharp scissors and hang them upside down in small bunches in a well-ventilated room to dry.

The spidery, six-pointed flowers have an almost metallic look to them

FLOWERHEAD ▶
20cm (8in)
across

DRAMA QUEEN

The outlandishly large, globe-like flowerheads of *Allium cristophii* draw attention to themselves in any garden, large or small. They spring up as if from nowhere and soon tower above their companions, grabbing attention away from all but the boldest flowers.

Flattened flowers provide easy access for bees

Euphorbias *EUPHORBIA*

WEIRD AND WONDERFUL, euphorbias make you either shudder or swoon – and although I admit I was once in the former camp, they're now one of my favourite architectural plants, as much for their showy petal-like bracts as for their sheer versatility. Despite their extraordinary, almost surreal appearance they are surprisingly easy to combine with other plants. Most are hardy herbaceous perennials and are happy in a wide range of conditions. They provide a really distinctive show from mid-spring right up until late summer.

FIRE BRIGHT
You couldn't find a better name than 'Fireglow' for this *Euphorbia griffithii*, with its smouldering orange-red bracts and red leaf veins.

ALL CHANGE
Like its namesake, *Euphorbia dulcis* 'Chameleon', with its rich purple leaves, blends in magically with surrounding colours in any shade of purple, red or green.

RAZZLE DAZZLE
Although the individual bracts of *Euphorbia palustris* are comparatively small, they are produced in such quantity that they create a mass of bright yellow.

The milky sap of euphorbias is a skin irritant, so take care when cutting back plants and wear gloves and long sleeves. If the sap comes into contact with your skin, wash it off immediately. Seek medical advice if you get the sap in your eyes. Avoid planting euphorbias near a pond that contains fish, as the fish may react adversely to the sap.

LEMON ZEST
The lemon-lime bracts of *Euphorbia polychroma* 'Candy' bring an intense and unusual splash of colour from mid-spring to late summer.

◄ FLOWER SIZE
3cm (1¼in)
across

GROWING EUPHORBIAS

PLANT PROFILE

Mainly hardy herbaceous perennials, although others are biennial or shrubby.

- SIZE 30cm–150cm (1–5ft).
- FLOWER COLOURS Red, orange, yellow, green.
- FLOWERING From mid-spring to late summer.
- SITE They prefer well-drained soil in sun, but will tolerate a wide range of soils and part shade.

Planting To get euphorbias off to a good start, add well-rotted compost to increase soil fertility.

Dividing Divide mature plants in spring or autumn. *Euphorbia polychroma* has a very woody crown, so lift the whole plant and cut it into sections using a knife or spade. You can also increase your plant stock from seed (sow seeds in spring in a cold frame), or take basal shoot cuttings in late spring and root in a cold frame.

Growing tip Most euphorbias will produce a second flush of growth if cut back hard after flowering and kept well watered and fed.

My favourites *Euphorbia amygdaloides* var. *robbiae*; *E. characias* subsp. *characias* 'Humpty Dumpty'; *E. c.* subsp. *wulfenii*, *E. c.* subsp. *w.* 'Lambrook Gold', *E. c.* subsp. *w.* 'Spring Splendour'; *E. dulcis* 'Chameleon'; *E. polychroma*. For a moist, shady site or even a bog garden, *E. griffithii* 'Dixter' and *E. g.* 'Fireglow' are ideal. As ground cover in light shade, try *E. polychroma* 'Candy' (syn. 'Purpurea').

OUT OF THIS WORLD *right*
One of the strangest and the most striking looking of the euphorbias is *Euphorbia characias* subsp. *wulfenii*. In no time at all this evergreen biennial produces a mass of blue-green whorls of foliage topped by large domes of yellowy-green bracts.

Peonies *PAEONIA*

HERBACEOUS PEONIES bring fleeting but unashamed luxury to the garden. Although their exquisitely silky blooms don't last very long, I couldn't bear to miss my annual brief romance with them – and their attractively divided foliage earns its ornamental keep for the rest of the season. Peonies, especially the deep pink or red form of *Paeonia officinalis*, form an integral part of any cottage garden-style planting. The young foliage often has a pinkish tinge to it and looks superb emerging close to crown imperials (*Fritillaria imperialis*). Alternatively, try underplanting with the small snakeshead fritillaries, miniature daffodils or crocuses.

DREAM TICKET
The closely packed, paper-thin pale pink petals of 'Sarah Bernhardt' would fulfil any little girl's fantasy of possessing a silken petticoat skirt fit for a fairy-tale princess.

BOWLED OVER
The wonderful creamy-coloured centre of 'Bowl of Beauty' is surrounded by a collar of shell-like pink petals.

WHITE GOLD
With a deep bowl of white around a dense mound of rich golden stamens, 'Krinkled White' is almost waterlily-like in beauty.

PINK FLUSH
The semi-double flowers of 'Auguste Dessert' have unusual bright pink petals, each one streaked with a darker pink.

ROYAL STANDARD
I love single, deep red peonies like this *Paeonia tenuifolia*; their central boss of golden stamens stands out with a truly regal air.

GROWING PEONIES

PLANT PROFILE
These are hardy perennials. For taller plants, consider the shrubby, or tree, peonies.

- SIZE Most 60–90cm (2–3ft).
- FLOWER COLOURS Red, pink, white, cream.
- FLOWERING Early summer.
- SITE Moisture-retentive yet well-drained soil, in full sun. Provide shade from early-morning sun following frosty nights.

Planting Incorporate plenty of well-rotted garden compost when planting. Do not bury the crowns more than 2.5cm (1in) beneath the surface or flowering will be reduced.

Dividing Divide established crowns in autumn, but only if really necessary as they resent disturbance.

Fantastic flowers Keep plants well watered and feed with sulphate of potash in spring and autumn.

Pruning Deadhead as soon as flowers fade. Cut back faded stems to the base in autumn.

Wilting If stems blacken at the base and then wilt, the fungal infection peony wilt is probably to blame. Remove all affected stems completely as soon as they are seen, cutting right back into the crown if necessary.

My favourites *Paeonia lactiflora* 'Bowl of Beauty', *P. l.* 'Duchesse de Nemours', *P. l.* 'Karl Rosenfield', *P. l.* 'Krinkled White' *P. l.* 'Président Poincaré'; *P. officinalis* 'Alba Plena', *P. o.* 'Lize van Veen', *P. o.* 'Rosea Plena', *P. o.* 'Rubra Plena'. For scent, try *P. lactiflora*, *P. l.* 'Félix Crousse', *P. l.* 'Sarah Bernhardt', *P. l.* 'Laura Dessert'.

Use ring stakes, canes or twiggy branches to support varieties of Paeonia lactiflora and plants in exposed sites.

Stems and leaves are often flushed with pink or red

Petals have slightly wavy edges or are indented

FLOWER SIZE ▶
10cm (4in)
across

PRINCE CHARMING
You might be forgiven for mistaking 'Arabian Prince' for a confectioner's exotic creation! With its screaming pink petals and rich yellow stamens, this peony demands attention wherever it is planted.

GOOD COMPANIONS *right*
Peonies are wonderful plants for herbaceous and mixed borders, where they can be combined easily with a wide range of herbaceous perennials, shrubs or climbers. In particular, they make marvellous companions for other showy flowers such as roses, delphiniums and alliums.

Sweet peas *LATHYRUS ODORATUS*

As subtle as a flouncy Belgian blind they may be, but most people will happily own up to a weakness for sweet peas. And why not? If you aren't seduced by their frilly, butterfly-like flowers in the loveliest colours imaginable, then you will be by their tremendous perfume. These fast-growing annual climbers are easy to raise from seed and will create a quick screen, clothe a wigwam or brighten up a shrub throughout the summer.

SCENTED HEAVEN
With its heavily scented, bluish-mauve flowers, 'Noel Sutton' is a favourite for which I can always find a place.

Delicate tendrils for attachment

Stems are elegantly winged

OF CABBAGES AND KINGS
This sweet pea was picked fresh from my garden. I like to grow them in amongst the vegetables so that I can harvest the crops and flowers together.

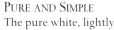

PURE AND SIMPLE
The pure white, lightly perfumed flowers of 'White Supreme' make long-lasting, elegant cut flowers.

OLD AND NEW
The bright, rose-pink flowers of 'Jayne Amanda' look equally good in a modern or traditional cottage garden.

FLOWER SIZE ▶
3.5cm (1½in) across

GROWING SWEET PEAS

PLANT PROFILE
Annual climbers.

• SIZE 90cm (3ft) is average; tall ones reach 1.8–3m (6–10ft), dwarf 15–30cm (6–12in).

• FLOWER COLOURS Red, orange, yellow, purple, lilac, pink, white, cream and bicolours.

• FLOWERING Throughout summer.

• SITE Moist, fertile soil, in full sun or part shade.

Soil Preparing the ground before sowing or planting is essential. The soil must be kept constantly moist if the sweet peas are to continue to flower throughout the season. Dig in plenty of organic matter, such as well-rotted horse manure or garden compost, to encourage soil moisture retention.

Sowing seeds Sow seed in mid-autumn or early spring. The seed coats of the black or mottled seeds are tough and germination is more reliable and quick if you nick the seed coat opposite the "eye" first. Seeds can either be sown in pots or

trays or in special sweet pea tubes (these allow you to grow the plants on and transplant them with minimum root disturbance). To encourage good, bushy growth, pinch out the growing tips of the seedlings once they have two pairs of leaves. Harden off and plant out in mid- to late spring.

Watering Regular watering is the key to success. Good soil preparation will make this an easier task, but even then sweet peas need plenty of moisture if they are to flower constantly and for the maximum possible length of time.

Plant problems Sweet peas are prone to a range of fungal diseases that build up in the soil, so always choose a fresh site every year.

Support Sweet peas must have some support. Their tendrils will cling to netting, wires, canes, twiggy branches or shrubs.

My favourites 'Blue Mantle', 'Cambridge Blue', 'Catherine', 'Charles Unwin', 'Daphne', 'Diamond Wedding', 'Midnight', 'Milestone', 'Noel Sutton', 'Old Times', 'Painted Lady', 'Patio Mixed', 'Pulsar', 'White Supreme'.

HIGH CLIMBERS *above*
For a simple yet attractive feature, grow sweet peas up a frame of twiggy sticks or canes in the border or, if space is limited, in a container, where they will quickly create a mass of colour.

MIXED MEDLEY *right*
Sweet peas come in pastel or dark shades, pure colours or bicolours, to suit all tastes. They look especially charming when many colours are grown together.

Sowing in individual tall pots keeps root disturbance to a minimum when planting. Better still, choose paper or fibre pots that disintegrate in the soil.

Tulips *TULIPA*

THE NATURAL
Less showy than many of the cultivated varieties, *Tulipa kurdica* produces a subtle, natural-looking display.

THE DAYS OF "TULIP MANIA" may be over, but using tulips is still a splendid way to create a bright splash of colour early in the year. They come in a wide range of shapes and colours, to suit every whim and location. Tulips are often thought of as too much bother, because it is best to lift, store and replant their bulbs every year. However, it is often worth experimenting and leaving them in the ground; some may reappear for several years. *Tulipa kaufmanniana* is one of the most reliable repeat performers.

AMONG CHAMPIONS
The bright yellow petals of 'Olympic Flame' are streaked orange-red; they look fantastic among red or yellow wallflowers.

HIDDEN VIRTUES *right*
Forget-me-nots (*Myosotis*) go well with many tulips. As an added bonus, their foliage masks the tulip leaves as they age and fade.

MYSTIQUE OF THE EAST
Tulip petals have beautiful textures; the silky, pale purple petals of 'Arabian Mystery' are edged in delicate white lace.

GROWING TULIPS

PLANT PROFILE

Not reliably perennial; ideally, lift bulbs as foliage dies, store in a shed then replant.

- SIZE 10–60cm (4–24in).
- FLOWER COLOURS Red, orange, yellow, green, purple, lilac, pink, white, cream.
- FLOWERING Spring.
- SITE Light or medium soil, preferably alkaline, in sun or part shade, ideally in a sheltered position.

Planting Varies with bulb size, but usually about 15cm (6in) deep. On sandy soils, plant bulbs even deeper than this. To make formal-looking blocks of colour, plant the bulbs only 10cm (4in) apart and in straight rows. Plant in late autumn, no earlier. This will greatly reduce the risk of them succumbing to tulip fire, a disfiguring and potentially fatal fungal disease.

Lifting You can plant bulbs in open-sided baskets (e.g. pond baskets) or mesh bags so that they can be lifted easily at the end of flowering. Allow the foliage to die back before storing.

Dividing Divide congested clumps after flowering, when the foliage has yellowed. Separate off any offsets, then replant both. Remember that offsets will take several years to reach flowering size.

My favourites 'Apeldoorn', 'Apricot Beauty', 'Attila', 'Ballerina', 'Cassini', 'Estella Rijnveld', *T. fosteriana, T. kaufmanniana, T. kurdica,* 'Olympic Flame', 'Orange Emperor', 'Oxford', Parrot Group, 'Queen of Night', 'Red Emperor', 'Red Riding Hood', *T. saxatilis*, 'Scarlet Baby', 'Shirley', 'Showwinner', *T. sprengeri,* 'Stresa', 'Toronto', 'Waterlily'.

At the end of the season, as the foliage yellows, lift tulips, loosen off soil and store them in a cool, frost-free shed.

REGAL FLAME
The flowers of 'Orange Monarch' have a fiery glow, but look inside and you will see purple anthers set against apricot-orange petals.

TWIST AND SHOUT
Love them or hate them, the crazy flowers of Parrot tulips are always eye-catching, as the bright, frilly 'Flaming Parrot' proves.

PRETTY IN PINK
The purple-pink blooms of 'Attila' may be very simple, but their elegance and sheer prettiness makes them a favourite with me.

GOLD STANDARD
If you want to grow a truly classic tulip, try 'Golden Apeldoorn'. It is taller than most; peek inside to see the black bases of the petals.

BABY LOVE *right*
Planted *en masse*, the low-growing 'Scarlet Baby' creates a stunning display.

FLOWER SIZE ▶
7.5cm (3in)
across

DARK STAR
The lovely, deep maroon flowers of 'Queen of Night' make me wonder why people still search for the elusive black tulip.

TULIP LILY *above*
One glance at any variety in the Kaufmanniana Group makes it clear why these are also known as water-lily tulips.

Irises *IRIS*

IRIS WAS THE GREEK GODDESS of the rainbow, and there are irises across the entire colour spectrum to justify that name. Some have delicate blooms in muted shades, others are brazen attention-seekers in bold bronzes and purples. You can grow irises almost anywhere in the garden; although most need a free-draining, sunny position, some, such as *Iris unguicularis* and *I. sibirica,* prefer a moist spot in light shade. Irises continue to bloom long after other spring flowers have faded, providing colour before herbaceous borders come into their own.

BARE-FACED BRILLIANCE *above*
'Shirley Pope' is what is known as a beardless iris – as you might well expect from her name! I've always loved this classic iris.

Try to control slugs and snails around irises, as their feeding damage encourages the development of rhizome rot, a potentially fatal iris disease.

Iris leaves may be marred by pale brown spotting due to fungal leaf spot disease. This usually develops towards the very end of summer, so just snip off the worst-affected leaves. If the problem is severe, spray with a suitable fungicide.

HEIGHT OF FASHION
Between late spring and the start of summer the tall, demure, pinky-lilac iris 'Carnaby' stands nearly waist-high in the border.

LOWER THE FLAG
Perfect for smaller gardens or towards the front of a border, the miniature bearded iris 'Joette' is half the height of 'Carnaby'.

GOOD VIBRATIONS *left*
Not two colours I would combine on my walls or in my wardrobe, but 'Brown Lasso' has real style.

INNER GLOW *right*
If you can position irises so that their petals are illuminated by the sun, they will take on a translucence that suggests that they are glowing from within.

FLOWER SIZE ▶
10–13cm (4–5in) across

GROWING IRISES

PLANT PROFILE

Hardy perennials.

- SIZE Most 25–90cm (10–36in).
- FLOWER COLOURS Pink, orange, yellow, blue, purple, lilac, white, cream, brown.
- FLOWERING Most late spring to early or mid-summer; *Iris unguicularis* autumn to spring.
- SITE Most prefer sandy or free-draining loam, neutral to alkaline, in full sun.

Planting Plant rhizomes in late summer or autumn; early spring is also acceptable. If possible, dig in some very well-rotted manure – but as iris roots are easily scorched, this must be done several weeks before planting or not at all. Plant rhizomes 38cm (15in) apart, with the surface of each rhizome *just* above ground level and preferably facing the sun to ensure maximum exposure to sunlight. Trim back any leaves by about half to reduce the risk of wind rock loosening the young roots. Keep the rhizomes well watered for a couple of weeks after planting to encourage establishment. Feed in autumn with the kind of fertilizer called "superphosphates" or any product high in phosphate.

Dividing Divide established clumps in autumn after the foliage has died back.

My favourites 'Amethyst Flame'; 'Antarctic'; 'Big Day'; 'Black Knight'; 'Blue Smoke'; *Iris ensata*; 'Fiery Song'; *I. foetidissima*; 'Gerald Darby'; 'Langport Pansy'; 'Langport Sultan'; 'Langport Wren'; 'Lothario'; 'Perry Hill'; 'Saint Crispin'; 'Smart Girl'; 'The Monarch'; *I. sibirica* 'Dreaming Yellow'; *I. s.* 'Papillon', *I. s.* 'Sparkling Rosé', *I. s.* 'White Swirl'; *I. unguicularis.*

BRONZED ADONIS *right*
Although striking plants of great stature, irises also merit closer examination to appreciate the fine detailed markings and colour finishes of petals. Here, 'Bronze Cloud' takes on almost rainbow-like colours.

Lilies *LILIUM*

WHETHER GROWING in a border or container, lilies always look elegant, stately, and perhaps just a tiny bit aloof. Their striking good looks, often combined with a gorgeous scent, make them a real favourite. They are easy to grow if given well-drained soil and a little (but not too much) shade. Even if you are restricted to a backyard or balcony, you can fill it with the intense colours and scents of lilies, as many of them thrive in pots and tubs.

HEAVENLY TRUMPETS
The delicious fragrance of *Lilium longiflorum* is paradisiacal. Add to this its elegant flowers, and it's close to perfection!

QUEEN OF LILIES
With its heady perfume and striking purple or purple-brown markings, *Lilium regale* deserves a prominent position.

PEAK OF PERFECTION
I love the texture of pale lily petals; those of 'Mont Blanc' look like satiny slopes of whipped cream.

CRIMSON CUPS
Place a pot or two of the dazzling 'Red Night' in the early summer border to bring a colour scheme to life.

GROWING LILIES

PLANT PROFILE

Bulbs that flower every year: lift and store half-hardy lily bulbs over winter.

• SIZE Most 60–120cm (2–4ft); some up to 3m (10ft).

• FLOWER COLOURS Red, orange, yellow, purple, lilac, pink, white, cream, brown.

• FLOWERING Early, mid- or late summer.

• SITE Fertile soil; part shade or sun, depending on variety.

Planting Early spring, or autumn to flower the following summer. Bulbs establish better if soaked in tap water for an hour before planting. It's important to plant deep enough, especially stem-rooting lilies – *Lilium longiflorum, L. martagon, L. regale.* Dig in plenty of well-rotted horse manure or garden compost to a depth of at least 20cm (8in), then plant the bulbs 10–15cm (4–6in) deep. Plant *L. candidum* and *L. cernuum* more shallowly, in about 10cm (4in) of soil.

Soil Rich but well-drained. Lilies are heavy feeders, so add plenty of compost or well-rotted horse

manure, or use a proprietary feed. Over-wet soil conditions, especially in a poorly drained container, cause the bulbs to die off rapidly, so ensure drainage is very good. In clay soil, set bulbs on a layer of grit or sharp sand 2.5cm (1in) deep.

Watering Although lilies cannot bear damp feet, they need a steady supply of moisture throughout the growing period, so regular watering is essential when the weather is dry.

Dividing Established clumps of lilies should be divided every three or four years.

Lilies in containers Most lilies do well in pots: try 'Casablanca', 'Mont Blanc', 'Pink Perfection', 'Red Carpet' or *Lilium speciosum* var. *album.* Three bulbs per 25–30cm (10–12in) pot of a loam-based compost such as John Innes No. 2 works well. Drainage must be good, so use lots of crocks in the base of the pot.

My favourites 'African Queen', 'Acapulco', *Lilium candidum, L. grayi,* 'Liberation', *L. longiflorum* especially *L. l.* 'White American'), 'Magic Pink', *L. martagon,* 'Mont Blanc', 'Red Night'; 'Star Gazer' – to be honest, I like most lilies!

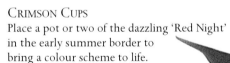

Most lilies are fully hardy, but some, like Lilium longiflorum (above), can be harmed by cold. Grow these in containers and move to a frost-free position over winter.

RED-HOT CHILLI *right*
The dashing 'Acapulco' has a powerful fragrance to match its striking red blooms. Here, it adds a touch of spice to a border of purples and pinks, which includes roses, foxgloves, irises, veronicas, cosmos, dicentras and aquilegias. Try to position scented varieties where you can enjoy the full benefit of their perfume: on or next to a terrace or patio, or by a garden seat, arbour, open window or frequently used path.

A STAR IS BORN *left*
With almost no effort on your part, the red-flushed 'Star Gazer' can be a real hit in mid-summer. It's great in containers, has a delicate fragrance and, like most lilies, it makes an excellent cut flower.

Many lilies have delicately patterned petals

Take care that lily pollen does not get onto fabrics — the stain is difficult to remove

FLOWER SIZE ▶
18cm (7in) across

Taller varieties may need some support, particularly in exposed sites

Distinctive stamens come in a range of contrasting and complementary hues

Feathery & light

PICTURE SUMMER SKIES, STUDDED WITH WISPS OF FEATHER-LIGHT CLOUDS . . . IT MUST BE MORE THAN COINCIDENCE THAT WHENEVER I WANT TO CREATE DREAMY DRIFTS OF COLOUR, I NEARLY always think of flowers in shades of blue, mauve and white, often with blue-grey tinted foliage. The flowers in this section are themselves mostly quite small, but it is not their individual form, size or colour that make them so worthwhile. By all means enjoy their demure, delicate features close up, but they truly come into their own when grown *en masse*, forming a billowing haze that is lovely in its own right, or when it is used to link flowers with stronger colours and forms in a subtle, easy manner. Some, in particular cornflowers and nigellas, are ideal where you need some temporary, light "fillers" while permanent plants become established.

"At the height of summer, nigellas form a haze of vivid blues and purples, taking the heat out of the flower border."

NIGELLAS, PAGES 72–3

Left NIGELLAS (PP.72–3), BRINGING CLOUDS OF SOFT BLUE TO THE SUMMER BORDER

Cornflowers CENTAUREA

I CAN'T THINK of a more perfect cross between a wild and a cultivated flower than cornflowers. They are such a quick and easy way to bring a bright splash of colour to a border or container, and many perennial forms are terrific value, flowering from early to mid-summer and then producing a second flush of blooms in the autumn. Even when they are not in flower, their foliage, which is often silvery grey, acts as a foil for other plants close by.

BLACK AND WHITE
With its prominent dark stamens and fine, feathery petals, *Centaurea montana* f. *alba* combines great sturdiness with a fragile elegance.

PINK POMPON
Some cornflowers have very densely packed petals that form tight rosettes, such as this *Centaurea cyanus* 'Tall Rose', an unusual pink form.

SUMMER HEAT
Cornflowers with pinky colours such as this carmine *Centaurea dealbata* 'Steenbergii' will instantly bring a warm glow to any border or planting.

WHITE RELIEF
Delicate white markings, either frilling the edges of the petals or, as here on this *Centaurea cyanus*, brightening up their bases, are characteristic of cornflowers.

INTO THE BLUE *right*
Centaurea cyanus looks most striking when it is planted closely together to produce a mass of brilliant blue. Like all cornflowers, it makes a pretty cut flower.

WILL O' THE WISP
Centaurea montana 'Pasham's Purple' has a timeless grace, with its very slender, pinky-lilac petals and intricately patterned sepals.

GROWING CORNFLOWERS

PLANT PROFILE

Hardy annuals, biennials and perennials.

• SIZE Most grow to 20–45cm (8–18in); some varieties may reach 90cm (3ft).

• FLOWER COLOURS Red, yellow, blue, purple, lilac, pink, white.

• FLOWERING From early summer to autumn.

• SITE Any well-drained soil, in full sun.

Sowing annuals Sow seeds of annuals direct into the ground in early autumn or early to mid-spring. Make several sowings throughout the spring to ensure a display of flowers for several months.

Growing perennials Sow seeds of perennials in spring, in pots or trays in a cold frame. Prick out, pot on, then plant in a spare piece of ground outside until autumn, when they should be ready to be planted in the border. You can also take cuttings, divide established plants about every three years, or buy small plants if you want to make a head start.

Soil Cornflowers will grow in any well-drained soil, as long as it is kept well fed. On heavy sites it is worth incorporating plenty of grit or even planting on a slight mound to ensure better drainage.

Position Make sure that the site is sunny; without enough sunlight, flowering will be poor and the plants will become rather leggy.

My favourites *Centaurea cineraria, C. cyanus, C. hypoleuca* 'John Coutts', *C. macrocephala, C. montana* f. *alba, C. moschata* (syn. *Amberboa moschata*), 'Pulchra Major' (syn. *Leuzea centauroides*).

If you want to encourage wildlife, cornflowers are ideal, attracting both bees and butterflies into the garden.

•

Grow the mat-forming Centaurea bella in a sunny spot and you will be able to enjoy a silver-grey carpet of foliage topped with bright pinkish-lilac flowers from late spring to mid-summer.

Tiny petals are packed closely together to form little mop-heads

FIELD OF DREAMS
Here, vibrant blue cornflowers look superb combined with godetia and Californian poppies in bright, contrasting shades of pink and orange.

◀ FLOWER SIZE
4cm (1½in) across

Intricately patterned spherical buds

Eryngiums *ERYNGIUM*

IF THERE IS ONE PLANT that could conceivably have come from another planet, it's eryngium – their flowerheads really do look like outlandish spacecraft. All of them have a bright, almost metallic coloration to their leaves, stems, flowers and spiky bracts. Most are hardy and herbaceous, a few are evergreen, and all flower constantly for most of the summer. They are an easy way to bring fast-growing colour and really unusual texture and form into the garden. Given plenty of sun and a well-drained soil, they thrive with only very little attention.

TRUE STEEL
The vibrant, glistening, steely blue of *Eryngium alpinum* brings a metallic sheen to the border. To intensify the colour, try underplanting with purples and blues.

TREASURE FROM THE DEEP
The flowers of *Eryngium variifolium* look as if they have been dried, however fresh they are. Their silvery, spider-like appearance reminds me of a deep-sea creature.

SPIKY SOUVENIR
Eryngium giganteum is sometimes called Miss Willmott's Ghost. It appeared mysteriously in every garden that this great plantswoman visited; she was suspected of scattering seed.

GROWING ERYNGIUMS

PLANT PROFILE
Hardy perennials.
- SIZE Most 60–150cm (2–5ft); *Eryngium pandanifolium* will grow to a lofty 2.4m (8ft).
- FLOWER COLOURS Green, white, blue, purple, lilac; many have a silvery, almost metallic cast to them.
- FLOWERING Throughout the summer.
- SITE Ideally, well-drained soil and plenty of sun.

Soil Eryngiums will survive in all but the heaviest soils, but to thrive they need good drainage. When planting, work handfuls of grit into the planting area if your soil is not very free-draining.

Position Without plenty of sun their growth becomes spindly and their metallic colours turn dull.

Sowing seeds Some eryngiums can be raised from seed. Sow in spring, then plant out in autumn.

Cuttings Take root cuttings (see p.41) in late winter.

Dividing You can divide large plants in the autumn or spring.

Protection Cold, damp conditions over winter can kill these otherwise tough plants by encouraging rotting of the crown. Clearing all plant debris from the crown in autumn and mulching with a light, dry material such as chipped bark will help to stop this on a less-than-perfect site.

Drying The flowerheads are striking in dried indoor arrangements and are best collected on a dry day and suspended in a well-ventilated shed or garage to dry.

Planting partners Early spring bulbs such as crocuses make excellent companions for eryngiums. The bulbs will have finished flowering by the time the eryngiums have got moving, so neither cramps the other's style. Once the eryngiums have put on growth, they look stunning close to flowers with blue or lilac colouring, or a contrasting white.

My favourites *Eryngium agavifolium*; *E. alpinum*; *E. bourgatii*, *E. b.* 'Oxford Blue'; *E. giganteum* (Miss Willmott's Ghost); *E. × oliverianum*; *E. proteiflorum*; *E. × tripartitum*; *E. variifolium*.

Prominent grey-white
veins are characteristic

Showy, silvery-grey
bracts form a ruff around
the flowerhead

Minute flowers
are grouped into
a dense mound

Bees and butterflies both find
eryngiums very attractive, and
on warm, sunny days the
flowerheads hum with activity.

SPINE TINGLER
Between mid-summer and early
autumn *Eryngium × oliverianum* is
covered in purple flowerheads.
Like all eryngiums, it makes a
good flower for arrangements
if the stems are cut before the
flowers are fully opened.

◄ FLOWER SIZE
6cm (2½in)
across

Lavender *LAVANDULA*

A HAZE OF PURPLE, the buzzing of bees and, above all, that wonderful sun-baked fragrance – if anything says "summer" to my senses, it's lavender. Provided there's a dry, sunny spot for them, they suit every garden style imaginable. For an early start to the season, grow traditional English lavenders (*Lavandula angustifolia*) – but be sure to make room, too, for the more unusual French lavender (*L. stoechas*) varieties.

TOUCH OF CLASS
The compact shape and rich colour of *Lavandula angustifolia* 'Hidcote' make it perfect for creating a classic English garden edging for a path or border.

IN THE PINK
The subtle, whisper pink of *Lavandula angustifolia* 'Loddon Pink' creates a delicate haze of colour and perfume in any sunny spot from mid- to late summer.

THE CLASSIC, *above and right*
In mid-summer the mounded, grey-green form of *Lavandula angustifolia* 'Twickel Purple' is brought to life by countless slender purple flower spikes.

GROWING LAVENDER

PLANT PROFILE

Hardy to half-hardy; grow tender types in a sheltered position or provide winter protection.

- SIZE 25cm–75cm (10–30in) tall, depending upon variety.
- FLOWER COLOURS Blue, purple, lilac, pink, white.
- FLOWERING From late spring throughout summer.
- SITE The poorer and drier the soil the better, in full sun.

Soil Lavenders need a very well drained (preferably limy) soil and lots of sun. They thrive on poor soil, and need very little feeding.

Pruning Regular trimming in mid-spring is a must to prevent plants becoming thin and straggly. Combine this with a very light pruning in autumn to remove faded flower spikes, and the plants should remain compact for several years. If grown as hedging, clip into shape in mid-spring. Even with regular pruning, lavenders usually lose their shape and charm after eight or nine years, and are best replaced.

Cuttings Take semi-ripe cuttings in late spring or late summer: a cheap and easy way to make lots of plants for edging.

Containers In cold areas, grow less hardy lavenders in well-drained containers, and move into a frost-free greenhouse or porch over winter.

My favourites *Lavandula angustifolia* 'Twickel Purple'; *L. × intermedia* Dutch Group, *L. × i.* 'Grappenhall'; *L. stoechas, L. s.* f. *leucantha, L. s.* subsp. *pedunculata.* For miniature hedging to edge paths, use *L. angustifolia* 'Hidcote', *L. a.* 'Loddon Pink' or *L. a.* 'Nana Alba'.

CRAZY CHARM *below*
A lavender that has jumped into the dressing-up box and emerged wearing a chief's headdress, *L. stoechas* has a much zanier appeal than its chic common name, French lavender, might suggest. It is slightly more tender than most other lavenders, but if you choose your site carefully it's not difficult to keep over cold winters.

COLOUR COORDINATION *above*
The grey-blue roof and pale blue walls of a nearby house are brought to life by the grey-green foliage and purple flowers of the lavender growing nearby.

Bright pinkish-purple feather-like bracts

FLOWERHEAD ▶
5cm (2in)
tall

The tiny flowers are almost overshadowed by showier bracts

To dry lavender, cut the flower spikes before the flowers are fully open and hang them in bunches upside down in a well-ventilated shed or room.

Nigellas *NIGELLA*

AT THE HEIGHT OF summer, nigellas form a haze of vivid blues and purples, taking the heat out of the flower border. Their delicate flowers and feathery foliage give them a dream-like quality, but despite their fragile appearance they are one of the easiest annuals to grow from seed, and as they are fully hardy they can be sown direct in spring or the previous autumn. Nigellas make lovely cut flowers. Their drying seedheads add interest to the border for weeks, or can be cut and brought indoors for dried flower arrangements.

JEWEL COLOURS
Introduce a touch of the exotic with the seed mixture Persian Jewel (*above, right, and opposite*). With pretty blooms in deep violet-blue, sky-blue, rose-pink, deep pink and white, they shine, gem-like, all summer and right up until the first frosts.

▼ FLOWER SIZE
4cm (1½in)
across

COTTAGE-GARDEN FAVOURITES
Nigellas make attractive gap-fillers in a perennial flower border. Here, they contribute to a cottage-garden feel, together with foxgloves, peonies, campanulas and gypsophila.

GROWING NIGELLAS

PLANT PROFILE

Hardy annual: sow seed each year, or allow plants to self-seed at will.

• SIZE 40–50cm (16–20in); dwarf forms 20–25cm (8–10in).

• FLOWER COLOURS Yellow, blue, purple, lilac, pink, white.

• FLOWERING Through summer and into early autumn; sow in autumn for an early start.

• SITE Ideally, sandy or well-drained soil, in full sun.

Planting Seeds can be sown directly into the flowerbed in autumn or spring, then thinned once the seedlings have appeared. Spring sowings are generally more reliable. Plants usually take 10 to 12 weeks to reach flowering size.

Self-seeding Nigellas spring up everywhere! Move self-sown seedlings, if necessary, as soon as they are large enough to handle in the spring. Flower colour may not be exactly the same as last year's plants.

Soil I find that nigellas will tolerate everything but heavy soil.

Dwarf varieties For superb border or path edging, you can't beat the very compact 'Dwarf Moody Blue' or 'Shorty Blue', which reach a height of about 25cm (10in). They are also ideal for containers.

My favourites *Nigella hispanica*; *N. damascena*, *N. d.* 'Miss Jekyll Azure Blue', *N. d.* 'Miss Jekyll Alba', *N. d.* 'Mulberry Rose', *N. d.* 'Red Jewel', *N. d.* Persian Jewel Series, *N. d.* 'Oxford Blue'. I'm intrigued by the seedheads of *N. orientalis* 'Transformer'. Turn them inside out to make silvery buff-coloured "flowers" for indoor displays.

To stop nigellas self-seeding, pick the seedheads just as they start to open and collect the seed to sow elsewhere.

Salvias *SALVIA*

THE MEDITERRANEAN ORIGINS of herbaceous salvias make them easy to grow on dry, sunny sites, often in situations where other plants would have difficulty surviving. These tall, slender, elegant perennials are quite different from the stocky little red salvias used as bedding plants and the bushy sages grown as cooking herbs, although several have aromatic leaves and all have the same basic flower form and clear, bright flowers. Some need care and a little work to take them through cold winters, but several are fully hardy; for these, winter wet is a greater enemy than low temperatures.

Individual flowers in tiers create a "cakestand" effect

SEA SPRITE *left*
Between summer and autumn, the delicate spikes of *Salvia coccinea* 'Coral Nymph' are studded with coral-coloured blooms.

DEPTH CHARGE *right*
Combine the dense, lilac-blue flower spikes of *Salvia × superba* with bright pink poppies for a truly electrifying display.

GROWING SALVIAS

PLANT PROFILE

The salvias described here are half-hardy to fully hardy perennials.

• SIZE 45–75cm (18–30in).

• FLOWER COLOURS Blue, purple, lilac, red, white.

• FLOWERING Early summer to early autumn.

• SITE Good drainage is vital, and lots of sun. For less hardy salvias, choose a sheltered spot away from cold winds.

Sowing seeds Perennial salvia species (not the varieties) can be raised from seed, and this is best done by sowing direct into open ground in the spring.

Dividing Established plants can be divided in spring.

Cuttings Where half-hardy plants are unlikely to survive the winter, take softwood cuttings in late spring and then overwinter the young plants in a frost-free cold frame or greenhouse. Harden off before planting out in late spring the following year.

Pruning It's a good idea to give hardy salvias a bit of a trim after flowering, removing all the faded flower spikes. This usually stimulates a second flush of flowers, at the end of summer or in early autumn. Frost may damage stems, especially of half-hardy salvias. Cut these back in spring.

My favourites Hardy types: *Salvia coccinea* 'Coral Nymph'; *S. nemorosa* 'Ostfriesland', *S. n.* 'Lubecca'; *S. × superba*; *S. verticillata*, *S. v.* 'Alba'. Half-hardy types: *S. farinacea*, *S. f.* 'Alba', *S. f.* 'Victoria'; *S. involucrata*; *S. patens* 'Cambridge Blue'; *S. uliginosa*.

For a changing display of colour, grow Salvia × superba, which has attractive reddish-purple bracts that persist on the plant after the lovely flowers have faded.

Although many salvias have pleasantly aromatic foliage, a few, in particular S. sclarea var. turkestanica, emit a distinctly unpleasant smell; sniff before you site them!

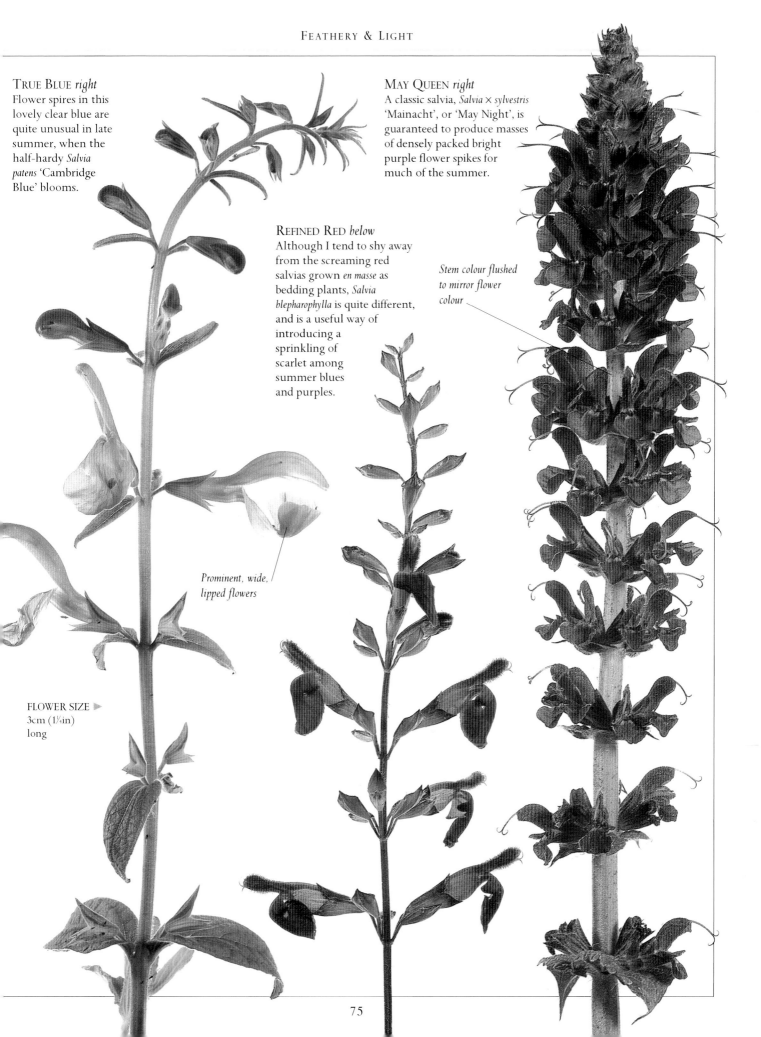

TRUE BLUE *right*
Flower spires in this lovely clear blue are quite unusual in late summer, when the half-hardy *Salvia patens* 'Cambridge Blue' blooms.

MAY QUEEN *right*
A classic salvia, *Salvia × sylvestris* 'Mainacht', or 'May Night', is guaranteed to produce masses of densely packed bright purple flower spikes for much of the summer.

REFINED RED *below*
Although I tend to shy away from the screaming red salvias grown *en masse* as bedding plants, *Salvia blepharophylla* is quite different, and is a useful way of introducing a sprinkling of scarlet among summer blues and purples.

Stem colour flushed to mirror flower colour

Prominent, wide, lipped flowers

FLOWER SIZE ▶
3cm (1¼in) long

Daisy shapes

ASK ALMOST ANYONE TO DRAW AN "INSTANT" PICTURE OF A FLOWER, AND THEY WILL PROBABLY SCRIBBLE DOWN A DAISY SHAPE. SIMPLE, EVEN CHILDISH IN FORM THEY MAY BE, BUT I cannot imagine a garden without some daisy-like flowers. I like them for their distinct personalities (think of a radiant sunflower, or of a quirky 'Whirligig' osteospermum) and for their sheer good-natured exuberance – these are the sort of flowers that simply lay themselves open to bask in the sun, and reflect their cheer and warmth back on to you! Even better, many of them bring glowing colours as summer ends. Where would we be without rudbeckias, asters and cosmos as the days start to cool and draw in? As if that were not enough, most of the plants featured in this section also provide great flowers for cutting so that you can enjoy their vibrance indoors too.

"With their irrepressibly cheerful flowers, sometimes as large as dinner plates . . . sunflowers always lift the spirits."

SUNFLOWERS, PAGES 82–3

Left RUDBECKIAS (PP.88–9), THEIR BRIGHT BLOOMS MAKING A GARDEN SEAT INVITING

77

Perennial asters *Aster*

LATE SUMMER AND AUTUMN wouldn't be the same without asters. Their brightly coloured flowers, usually with glorious, contrasting golden centres, bring warmth and colour into late autumn and give bees and butterflies a reason to linger in the garden. Herbaceous asters, sometimes called Michaelmas daisies, are best bought as plants, and although they are usually grown in borders, the more compact types also look great in containers or as border or path edging. Given a free-draining soil and plenty of sun, these hardy perennials are easy to grow.

PINK PERFECTION *left*
You'd probably only get away with a pink and yellow outfit at Ascot, but the semi-double *Aster novi-belgii* 'Little Pink Beauty' carries off its colour scheme with style anywhere.

DOUBLE IMPACT
The striking, double, dark pink flowers of *Aster novi-belgii* 'Patricia Ballard' remind me of chimney sweep's brushes atop their sturdy, long stems.

SWEET AND LOW *above*
From mid-summer to mid-autumn, *Aster lateriflorus* 'Horizontalis' produces masses of small, white or very pale pink flowers with prominent rose-pink centres.

SPLASH OF COLOUR *left*
Without the pink and purple mounds of colour produced by the asters – as exuberant and flamboyant as old-fashioned Sunday hats – this border would be quite subdued.

BLUE DELIGHT
For a less strident-looking aster choose the delicate, lilac-blue spidery flowers of *Aster × frikartii* 'Wunder von Stäfa'. It may need staking or supporting with twiggy sticks.

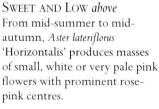

GROWING ASTERS

PLANT PROFILE

Hardy perennials.

- SIZE 45–150cm (18–60in).
- FLOWER COLOURS Blue, purple, lilac, pink, white, usually with contrasting yellow centres.
- FLOWERING Mid-summer until late autumn (or until the first frosts).
- SITE Preferably fertile and well-drained, alkaline or only slightly acid soil, in full sun.

Dividing Divide established plants every three or four years, ideally in early spring, otherwise in autumn.

Sowing seeds Only the species asters can be raised from seed. Seed sown in spring should produce flowering plants the same autumn.

Plant problems To minimize the risk of powdery mildew, to which asters are prone, keep plants moist at the roots by adequate watering towards the end of summer and in early autumn. Mulching also helps, as does ensuring good air circulation by making sure plants are not crowded.

My favourites Aster amellus 'Brilliant', A. a. 'King George', A. a. 'Pink Zenith', A. a. 'Violet Queen'; A. divaricatus; A. ericoides 'Pink Cloud'; A. × frikartii 'Mönch', A. × f. 'Wunder von Stäfa'; A. lateriflorus 'Horizontalis', A. l. 'Prince'; A. novi-belgii 'Patricia Ballard', A. n-b. 'Winston S. Churchill'; A. thomsonii 'Nanus'.

The lovely Aster × frikartii 'Mönch' (here planted with rudbeckias) is one of the most mildew-resistant of asters.

FUNGUS FREE

Many asters are vulnerable to the dreaded powdery mildew disease; to avoid this, grow *Aster amellus* 'Blue King' or other *A. amellus* varieties, which have good resistance.

FLOWER SIZE ▶
3–5cm (1¼–2in) across

Argyranthemums *ARGYRANTHEMUM*

GIVEN THE CHOICE between argyranthemums and their close relatives chrysanthemums, I'd go for the former every time. Whether you grow them in beds, borders or containers, with a well-drained soil and plenty of sun they can be guaranteed to produce masses of wide-eyed, innocent, daisy-like flowers throughout the summer and often into autumn. Sadly, although they will withstand winters in a Mediterranean climate, they are not hardy in colder regions, and are usually treated as half-hardy perennials or as annuals. Nevertheless, their flowers are so reliable and so pretty, and their flowering period so long, that they are worth the effort of overwintering or raising from cuttings each year.

GROWING ARGYRANTHEMUMS

PLANT PROFILE

Half-hardy, woody-based perennials often grown as annuals.

- SIZE 30–50cm (12–20in).
- FLOWER COLOURS Yellow, pink, white.
- FLOWERING Throughout summer and into autumn.
- SITE Well-drained soil or compost and full sun are essential if you are to get the best possible display of flowers.

Planting Plant out only after any danger of frost is over. If necessary, improve drainage first, using grit and bulky organic matter.

Cuttings Semi-ripe cuttings, 5–10cm (2–4in) long, are best taken in late summer and then overwintered in a cool but frost-free greenhouse. You can also take softwood cuttings in spring. Always choose healthy, non-flowering shoots when taking cuttings.

Pruning No need to prune, but pinching out shoot tips forms well-branched, bushy young plants.

Flower care Regularly picking off dead flowers extends the flowering period, so deadhead as soon as any flowers fade.

Plant problems Leaf miners may attack foliage, but although the pale wiggly lines they produce may look unsightly, they do little harm to the plants.

My favourites 'Chelsea Girl' (white with yellow centres), 'Jamaica Primrose' (warm yellow), 'Snowflake' (pure white, semi-double), 'Vancouver' (deep pink with a prominent pink centre).

In sheltered spots in mild areas, you may be able to overwinter plants in cold-climate gardens, provided the soil never gets too wet and the crowns are mulched with a deep layer of chipped bark, bracken or straw.

For real impact, especially for a container, invest in an argyranthemum that has been trained as a standard.

CLASSIC WHITES *below*
Throughout summer and often early autumn, sometimes until first frosts, *Argyranthemum frutescens* is a mass of pretty white flowers.

Slim yet sturdy dark green stems hold flowers erect

◀ FLOWER SIZE
2cm (¾in)
across

Petals often curve back slightly and are marked with distinct ridges

CONTAINED JOY *above*
Their compact, upright habit makes argyranthemums perfect for containers. Here, they are combined prettily with petunias; deadhead both plants regularly.

STAR ATTRACTION *right*
These open, daisy-like flowers – here, 'Apricot Sunrise' – are a magnet for many insects, including bees and hoverflies, whose larvae are ravenous aphid-eaters.

CENTRE OF ATTENTION
Some argyranthemums have large, elaborate "anemone" centres. The vigorous 'Vancouver' has double, deep pink flowers fading to buff-pink with age.

CARIBBEAN CHARMER
The petals of 'Jamaica Primrose' are the colour of their spring-flowering namesake, but the golden centre of each flower adds a more exotic touch.

Sunflowers *HELIANTHUS*

WITH THEIR IRREPRESSIBLY cheerful flowers, sometimes as large as dinner plates, and their phenomenal rate of growth, sunflowers always lift the spirits. Easy to grow in sun or part-shade, traditionally they were flowers for children to raise in a corner of the kitchen garden – but today, they appear in the most sophisticated florists' arrangements.

One happy result is a widening choice of varieties for gardeners, in shades of yellow, red, buff or brown, often dusted with pinks and bronzes.

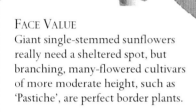

FACE VALUE
Giant single-stemmed sunflowers really need a sheltered spot, but branching, many-flowered cultivars of more moderate height, such as 'Pastiche', are perfect border plants.

MIXED BAG
One of the smaller sunflowers, 'Music Box Mixed' bears large numbers of very variably coloured, dark-centred flowers.

A HEAD START
For the impact of large flowers without the gigantic height that you would expect, 'Sunspot' is an excellent choice.

TARGET PRACTICE
The radiating blushes of colour on newer cultivars such as 'Pastiche' accentuate the giant central "landing pads" for bees.

GROWING SUNFLOWERS

PLANT PROFILE
The plants described here are all annuals – *Helianthus annuus*.
- SIZE 75cm–3m (30in–10ft).
- FLOWER COLOURS Yellows from lemon to gold; pink, red, buff, cream, brown.
- FLOWERING Throughout summer.
- SITE Sunflowers will grow in almost any soil, but for best results choose a heavy loam, in full sun or part shade.

Sowing seeds Growing sunflowers couldn't be simpler. Just clear the soil and sow the seeds direct, about 1cm (½in) deep, in spring. As their flowers will always turn towards the sun, make sure that you plant them in a position where you, and not the neighbours, will be able to enjoy them!

Plant care Young plants must be watered regularly, but once growing strongly sunflowers need very little attention. It is worth keeping them protected from the ravages of slugs, particularly when the plants are young.

Support If your garden is windy, you will either need to stake your sunflowers or choose 'Incredible' or 'Music Box', which are low-growing varieties.

For cutting Sunflowers make superb cut flowers; I always grow enough to bring some into the house. Cut them when they are coming into bud, then allow them to open out whilst in the vase, providing them with a cut-flower food. Most varieties will last for two to three weeks in water.

My favourites 'Giant Single', 'Incredible', 'Italian White', 'Moonwalker', 'Music Box', 'Sunbeam', 'Sunspot', 'Taiyo', 'Teddy Bear' and 'Velvet Queen'. For cut flowers, I choose the more branching cultivars of medium height, such as 'Pastiche', 'Prado Red', 'Prado Yellow', 'Valentine' and 'Toybox'.

SUN KING

The towering stems of 'Giant Single' are topped with huge flowers in a gorgeous, rich lemon yellow, their velvety russet-brown centres dusted with golden pollen.

◀ FLOWER SIZE
25cm (10in)
across

Kaleidoscopic golds and browns in the centre

Smaller flowers develop on short sideshoots

Ripe sunflower seeds are easily removed to keep for spring sowing or for feeding the birds during the winter months.

Cosmos *COSMOS*

THE DAISY-SHAPED flowers, long slender stems and fine, fern-like foliage of cosmos add up, quite simply, to perfection – the flowers are so faultless they look as if punched from plastic! Both the annuals and half-hardy perennials are easy to grow; they thrive in sunny, well-drained sites, even on the poorest soils, so are useful for creating splashes of colour where other plants would fail. The annuals can be raised from seed and will flower profusely from mid-summer onwards.

CHOCAHOLIC HEAVEN
Whether viewed *en masse* (*left*) or close up (*right*), the flowers of *Cosmos atrosanguineus* are truly sumptuous, and a quick sniff proves that the flowers really do smell of top-quality chocolate.

◀ FLOWER SIZE
4.5cm (1¾in) across

GROWING COSMOS

PLANT PROFILE

Annuals and perennials; they are not reliably hardy.

- SIZE 60–90cm (2–3ft).
- FLOWER COLOURS Red, orange, yellow, pink, white, brown.
- FLOWERING Throughout the summer until autumn, or the first frosts.
- SITE Best in a poor, sandy soil, in full sun; will perform quite well in semi-shade.

Sowing seed Annuals and some species can be sown from seed. Sow in a propagator at 16°C (61°F) in early spring, then harden off and plant out in late spring. Alternatively, sow *in situ* in late spring.

Cuttings *Cosmos atrosanguineus* and other half-hardy perennials can be grown from root cuttings (see p.41) in a propagator in early spring, or from basal cuttings taken in spring.

Fantastic flowers Regular deadheading ensures the largest flower size and longest possible flowering period.

Support It is often necessary to stake taller cosmos, especially if grown on richer soil.

Feeding Cosmos thrive in poor conditions, so avoid feeding; this may make them leggy and can even delay flowering.

My favourites *Cosmos bipinnatus* 'Daydream', *C. b.* 'Picotee', *C. b.* 'Sea Shells', *C. b.* 'Sensation', *C. b.* 'Tetra', *C. b.* 'Versailles'. The chocolate-scented *C. atrosanguineus* will bring delicious aromas into your garden. For exposed positions, *C. bipinnatus* 'Sonata', a dwarf variety, is ideal.

Grow cosmos in pots to brighten up terraces, patios and garden steps.

Cosmos make good cut flowers, so it's worth growing a few specifically for this purpose. The taller varieties are best for flower arranging, as their longer stems make them easier to display in a vase and combine with other flowers.

FLOWER SIZE ▶
7.5cm (3in)
across

SEASIDE TREAT *above*
The elaborate petals of the annual
Cosmos bipinnatus 'Sea Shells' bring a
dizzy splash of colour whether grown
in containers or in a border.

BEAUTY QUEEN *right*
The name cosmos comes
from the Greek *kosmos*,
meaning beautiful. Many
cosmos are good for
cutting – I like to bring
some indoors so that I can
take a closer look at the
lovely and intriguing
details of each bloom.

SUMMER SPIN *left*
Plant different varieties of *Cosmos
bipinnatus* in drifts for flowers
produced in profusion for much
of the summer, complete with a
backdrop of fine ferny foliage.

Osteospermums OSTEOSPERMUM

THE DIZZY PRETTINESS OF osteospermums is well worth the bit of extra effort that their tenderness demands in cool climates. Provided they have plenty of sun and a dry or free-draining soil, they will be covered in cheerful, daisy-like flowers throughout the summer months. Whether they are grown in containers or in a border, their striking, slightly clownish looks and crazy petal shapes are guaranteed to bring a smile to your face.

The centre reminds me of a honeycomb, with orange and brown bees clustered around it

WHITE WHIRL *right*
'Whirligig White' has an intriguing lilac flush to the petals and centre.

◀ FLOWER SIZE
5cm (2in)
across

PINK SENSATION *above*
The vibrant pink flowers of 'Stardust' burst out like stars in sunshine.

BUTTERY SPREAD *right*
Delicate creamy-yellow 'Buttermilk' has a serene presence in the border.

OUT OF AFRICA *above*
The dark centre of 'African Summer' contrasts with its grey-white petals.

WHIZ KID *right*
The startling outline of 'Whirligig Pink' is created by the pinched petal ends.

GROWING OSTEOSPERMUMS

PLANT PROFILE

Perennials, but they are not reliably hardy; bring plants into a protected spot over winter.

• SIZE 30–60cm (12–24in).
• FLOWER COLOURS Yellow, blue, purple, lilac, pink, white, cream.
• FLOWERING Throughout summer.
• SITE Free-draining soil, in full sun.

Planting A good range of named varieties should be available for sale as plants in spring and summer. As osteospermums tend to flop somewhat, grow in groups or plant close to other plants with a more attractive shape.

Soil A well-drained soil is essential. On heavier soils, plants are likely to grow poorly or die, even in mild weather. Incorporate plenty of grit in all but the most free-draining soils.

Sowing seeds Species can be raised from seed sown in late winter to early spring for flowering the following

summer. Sow them under glass and plant out after the last frosts. Propagate named varieties from semi-ripe cuttings taken towards the end of summer and then rooted in a sandy compost in a greenhouse.

Winter protection If you can't bring them under glass, they may survive frost with a deep mulch of straw, chipped bark or bracken, but drainage must also be good.

My favourites 'Blackthorn Seedling', 'Buttermilk', 'Cannington John', 'Pink Whirls', 'Silver Sparkler', 'Stardust', 'Whirligig'.

When grown next to a gravel path, osteospermums form excellent edging, and the gravel helps provide good drainage.

Rudbeckias *RUDBECKIA*

THE WONDERFULLY BOLD daisy shapes and rich flower colours of rudbeckias have an enduring appeal. In various shades of orange, yellow and brown, they bring a golden warmth to any border from summer right through until early autumn. They are very easy to grow, and although they prefer a fairly moist soil and plenty of sun, they still flower reasonably well even in light shade. In shadier conditions they tend to grow very tall, and if sunlight is in really short supply they may flop over, but the flowers will still keep coming. Named perennial varieties are best bought as young plants, but species and annuals can be raised from seed.

FOREVER GOLD *above*
From late summer until well into mid-autumn, *Rudbeckia fulgida* var. *speciosa* 'Viette's Little Suzy' is a mass of golden daisy flowers set against mid-green leaves.

SHORT BUT SWEET *right*
Usually grown as an annual, the lowish-growing *Rudbeckia hirta* 'Becky Mixed' produces a fine display in golds and browns.

SIGNS OF AUTUMN *left*
Like warm autumn sunshine, the bright yellow flowers and greeny-yellow centres of 'Herbstsonne' glow from mid-summer to early autumn. As they age the centres turn brown, a reminder that darker days are to follow.

GROWING RUDBECKIAS

PLANT PROFILE

Hardy annuals and perennials.

• SIZE Most 60–100cm (24–40in); *Rudbeckia laciniata* and its varieties can grow to 1.8m (6ft).

• FLOWER COLOURS Orange, yellow, brown.

• FLOWERING Throughout summer and into early autumn.

• SITE Fairly moist soil, with plenty of sun, although they will tolerate shade.

Planting It is possible to grow rudbeckias in soil that tends to become dry, but if they are to thrive you should incorporate plenty of bulky organic matter into the soil at planting, and regularly mulch and water them.

Invasiveness Watch out for *Rudbeckia laciniata* 'Hortensia' on fertile soils; it may become invasive.

Sowing seeds Sow seeds of annuals in early spring in a heated propagator. Harden off, then plant out in late spring or early summer.

Dividing Established perennials can be divided in either spring or autumn. In dry areas, autumn is preferable, as the soil tends to remain moister, giving newly divided plants longer to establish themselves before drying summer weather.

My favourites *Rudbeckia fulgida* var. *speciosa* 'Viette's Little Suzy'; *R. f.* var. *sullivantii* 'Goldsturm'; 'Goldquelle'; 'Herbstsonne' (also known as 'Autumn Sun'); *R. hirta* 'Goldilocks', *R. h.* 'Marmalade'; *R. laciniata* 'Hortensia' (also known as 'Golden Glow').

CROWD PLEASER
Rudbeckias make a cheerful contribution to any mixed planting, but for a really exuberant effect, try them alone in great masses, as here, crowding a garden bench – a really inviting place to sit!

POT OF GOLD
The flowers of *Rudbeckia fulgida* var. *sullivantii* 'Goldsturm' are larger than most and a rich, glowing yellowy-orange. It grows to about knee-high, and from a distance its flowers look like mounds of gold coins.

◄ FLOWER SIZE
up to 12cm (4½in) across

The taller rudbeckias, and those grown in a shaded position, often need staking, so to avoid this, grow varieties under 90cm (3ft) in height and choose a sunny spot.

•

Rudbeckias make great, long-lasting cut flowers for late summer and autumn.

•

Once the first flowering of Rudbeckia hirta is over, cut it back hard and feed it with liquid fertilizer to encourage a second flush of flowers.

Trumpets & bells

WE MAY NOT BE ABLE TO HEAR THE MUSIC THEY MAKE, BUT WHEREVER YOU SEE FLOWERS SHAPED LIKE TRUMPETS AND BELLS, YOU'LL HEAR THE BUZZING OF BEES, HUMMING AWAY TO THE sound of some silent symphony. Even the flowers themselves seem to be nodding and swaying along — it takes only a breath of wind to set them bobbing, bringing movement and life into the garden, as fascinating to watch as their busy visitors. The flowers here all share this animated elegance but, like the musical instruments they mimic, they vary considerably in tone. If dainty fritillaries and dicentras really belong to the players in some fairy orchestra, then bolder trumpets such as daffodils, and those where several flowers are grouped together on single stems, like agapanthus, look to me like a pretty powerful loudspeaker system!

"Late spring sees the arrival of fritillaries, their delicate flowers nodding in the slightest breeze."

FRITILLARIES, PAGES 100—101

Left CAMPANULAS (PP.96—7) BRING A REFRESHING BREATH OF THE MEADOW TO THE BORDER

91

Agapanthus *AGAPANTHUS*

THE NAME AGAPANTHUS comes from the Greek for "love flower", and I can't think of a more apt derivation for these beautiful blooms. They bring back happy memories of my travels to Madeira and South Africa, where they can be seen growing in huge numbers – an unforgettable sight. Agapanthus are readily available as plants (it takes several years for plants grown from seed to reach flowering size), and provided they are supplied with a moist, fertile soil and plenty of sun, they are easy to grow. They have a long flowering season, from mid-summer to early autumn, and most flower reliably for many years.

FIRM FAVOURITES *left* Amongst the more widely grown agapanthus are the Headbourne Hybrids, and they are also among the most reliably hardy.

GROWING AGAPANTHUS

PLANT PROFILE

Perennials; not reliably hardy, so winter protection may be necessary.

• FLOWER SIZE Most 60–90cm (2–3ft), but some may reach 1.1m (44in).

• FLOWER COLOURS Blue, purple, lilac, white.

• FLOWERING Mid-summer to early autumn.

• SITE Rich, moist soil, in full sun, sheltered from wind.

Planting Plant crowns 5cm (2in) below the soil surface in mid-spring.

Dividing Divide and replant in mid- to late spring. They don't like being disturbed, so try to keep clumps in one place and divide only when they are really congested.

Deadheading Cut back flowerheads once flowering is over, unless you are saving them for drying or a winter arrangement.

Frost protection A mulch, 10–15cm (4–6in) deep, is usually adequate. A free-draining material that remains relatively dry, such as chipped bark, is preferable to something that retains moisture around the crown. If necessary, hold the mulch in position using a covering of chicken wire. Plunge pots and containers or wrap them in a jacket of hessian, bubble wrap polythene or similar material.

My favourites 'Blue Giant', 'Bressingham Blue', 'Bressingham Bounty', 'Bressingham White', *Agapanthus campanulatus* 'Isis', Headbourne Hybrids, 'Lilliput'.

GRAND DESIGN *left*
With magnificent flowerheads
like these, it is no wonder
that agapanthus make
fabulous cut flowers.

HIDDEN CHARMS
In contrast to more showy
agapanthus, the discreet
charm of *Agapanthus inapertus*
lies in its drooping,
languorous, dark
purple flowers.

Individual
trumpet-shaped
blooms

◄ FLOWERHEAD
10cm (4in)
across

SUMMER SNOWFALL
When in full bloom in late
summer, the bell-shaped white
flowerheads of 'Snowy Owl'
resemble a mass of starry ice
crystals, bringing a cool note to a
late-season border.

*Agapanthus make elegant and
unusual edging for a wide
path, particularly one adjacent
to a fence or wall, where their
generous height will not dwarf
neighbouring plants.*

*Provided they are kept moist,
try growing agapanthus in
large containers; they look
great grown in pots with a hint
of blue in the glaze.*

BOLD BEDFELLOWS *right*
Agapanthus are no retiring
"wallflowers", and they need strong
forms and colours from their
companion plants to set them off.
Here, planted with yellowy-green
Cortaderia selloana 'Gold Band', a
golden conifer and boisterous
pinkish-red penstemons, the
agapanthus 'Loch Hope' makes a
particularly striking display.

Aquilegias *AQUILEGIA*

THESE PRETTY PERENNIALS ARE ALSO known as columbines, from the Latin *columbinus* – meaning dovelike – and the gentle flowers do indeed remind me of groups of doves, billing and cooing. Their fairy-tale quality is reinforced by delicate, almost feathery foliage – similar to that of the lovely maidenhair fern – for which alone they merit space in a border. Aquilegias are often quite short-lived, so expect to replace them every few years, or as soon as they start to lose vigour. They like a moist, well-drained soil, and will grow in sun or part shade.

◄ FLOWER SIZE
8cm (3¼in)
across

REAR VIEW *above*
The curving "spurs" behind aquilegia flowers are very well-developed on some varieties, as with this bright 'Crimson Star'.

SHADY PAIR *right*
The pale flowers of *Aquilegia vulgaris* combined with *Meconopsis cambrica* – Welsh poppies – bring a light touch to a shady corner of the garden.

PICK OF THE BUNCH
Among the taller aquilegias, the McKana hybrids are deservedly popular for their wide range of flower colours.

HAT TRICK
Aquilegia vulgaris and its varieties – here 'Adelaide Addison' – are known as "Granny's bonnet".

ICE MAIDEN *right*
The cool, translucent beauty of 'Dorothy' looks at its best in a shady spot.

GROWING AQUILEGIAS

PLANT PROFILE
Hardy perennials, although they are often short-lived.
- SIZE 30–90cm (12–36in).
- FLOWER COLOURS Red, yellow, blue, purple, lilac, pink, white, cream.
- FLOWERING Late spring to mid-summer.
- SITE Moist but well-drained soil; they will grow in full sun, but part shade suits them best.

Sowing seeds In early spring in a cold frame, or outdoors in summer. Don't transplant young seed-raised plants until the autumn.

Planting Add some leafmould to the soil when planting and you will be rewarded with plants that establish quickly and flower really well.

Dividing Established clumps of aquilegias can be divided in autumn or early spring.

Pruning Cut back flower stems after flowering if self-seeded plants are becoming a nuisance.

Self-seeding Aquilegias self-seed readily and usually re-establish very well when transplanted, so collect up seedlings and young plants from around the bases of their parents and use them to fill gaps elsewhere. Interesting "new" flower colour combinations may develop from these seedlings, since they will not be the same as the parent plant.

My favourites *Aquilegia caerulea*; *A. canadensis*, *A. c.* 'Nana'; 'Crimson Star'; 'Dorothy'; *A. formosa*; *A. fragrans*; *A. longissima*; 'Magpie'; McKana Group; 'Snow Queen'; *A. vulgaris*, *A. v.* 'Adelaide Addison', *A. v.* 'Nivea'.

The smaller alpine species and varieties are exquisite additions to rock gardens and troughs.

Campanulas *CAMPANULA*

ALL CAMPANULAS HAVE a lovely, relaxed, cottage-garden feel to them and, good-natured as they are, they will grow in most conditions. Some are a bit too eager – *Campanula portenschlagiana* and *C. poscharskyana* are very invasive, and will need to be clipped back regularly if you don't want them to swamp everything in sight. Campanulas are sometimes known as bellflowers (or "little bells", as the Latin name suggests). With some, the pointed petals curve back to form curled lips; in others, they open wide, making tiny stars.

GROWING CAMPANULAS

PLANT PROFILE

Most are hardy perennials.

- SIZE The range is huge, from low-growing forms just a few centimetres high to a statuesque 1.5m (5ft).
- FLOWER COLOURS Purple, blue, lilac, pink, white.
- FLOWERING Throughout summer.
- SITE They prefer a fairly well-drained soil, in sun or part shade.

Propagation Sow seed in mid-autumn or early to mid-spring in a cold frame or cold greenhouse. Pot on, and plant out one year later. Divide mature plants in autumn or spring.

Support Stake tall forms with twiggy sticks early in the season. In exposed gardens, grow shorter varieties to avoid having to stake.

Flower care Deadhead regularly to encourage further flowering.

My favourites *Campanula alliariifolia*; *C. carpatica* 'Chewton Joy', *C. c.* 'Bressingham White'; *C. lactiflora* 'Loddon Anna', *C. l.* 'Prichard's Variety', *C. l.* 'White Pouffe'; *C. latifolia* 'Gloaming'; *C. persicifolia*, *C. p.* 'Chettle Charm'; *C. poscharskyana* 'Blauranke'; *C. takesimana*.

FLOWER SIZE ▶
5.5cm (2¼in) long

GOOD ALL-ROUNDER *below*

The classic bell-shaped purple flowers of most campanulas not only look great in beds and borders, but they also make good cut flowers. They vary greatly in height, so can be used in anything from great blowzy bunches to perfect posies.

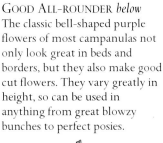

Flowers are visited by bees regularly

COUNTRY LASS

The elegant, pendulous pink and white bells of 'Elizabeth' are unlike those of most other campanulas, and bring a delicate touch to a cottage garden.

SUMMER MADNESS

Whether you like them or not, the near-spherical purple-violet globes produced by *Campanula glomerata* 'Superba' certainly create great impact in their own rather eccentric style.

PEACHY BEAUTY

The medium-sized *Campanula persicifolia* is sometimes known as the peach-leaved bellflower. It looks marvellous held above clumps of pale pink *Geranium × oxonianum* 'Wargrave Pink'.

Low-growing campanulas such as this Campanula portenschlagiana *can be allowed to fill gaps between paving or in walls, where they won't smother other plants.*

SIMPLY WILD *right*

Planted randomly, *Campanula persicifolia* helps to add colour and simple prettiness to a border based around wild flowers.

Dicentras DICENTRA

FROM THE MOMENT they appear above the ground in spring to the time they die back in late autumn, dicentras are a handsome addition to the garden. Their foliage, often feathery and fern-like, sometimes much divided, comes in many shades, from bright apple green to soft greyish-blue. The flowers are a knockout, dripping like jewels from poised, arching stems and, close up, exquisitely formed, from the tiny lockets of *Dicentra formosa* to the bolder bleeding hearts of *D. spectabilis*. These hardy perennials like a damp but well-drained soil, but apart from that will tolerate a range of growing conditions, from full sun to part shade. Although they may appear miserable in deep shade, they are more adaptable than one is often led to believe.

TRUE HEARTS
The unusually shaped pink and white flowers of *Dicentra spectabilis* look like miniature bleeding hearts clustered along the flower stem. They grace the border in spring and early summer.

GROWING DICENTRAS

PLANT PROFILE

Mostly hardy perennials.
- SIZE 30–75cm (12–30in).
- FLOWER COLOURS Red, yellow, purple, lilac, pink, white, cream.
- FLOWERING From mid-spring to late summer and into early autumn.
- SITE Prefer moist conditions in well-drained soil. Will grow in sun and part shade, and may even perform in deep shade.

Planting Add leafmould or well-rotted compost at planting to help encourage soil moisture retention.

Dividing You can divide well-established clumps between autumn and late winter, but try to avoid too much damage to the fragile crown or divisions are likely to fail. Discard old, woody parts.

Cuttings Take 7.5–10cm (3–4in) root cuttings (see p.41) in spring.

Place them in sandy compost or cuttings compost in a cold frame. Grow them on and plant out the following spring. This is the best way to propagate the fragile-rooted *Dicentra spectabilis* without disturbing it.

Sowing seeds Sow seed in spring at 15°C (59°F) and plant out in autumn, or in early spring the following year on heavier soils.

Self-seeding Dicentra hybrids self-seed readily, so if you don't mind growing specimens that may bear no resemblance to their parents, they are well worth keeping.

Planting associations The ferny foliage of any dicentra looks lovely in a slightly shaded spot among groups of hardy ferns.

My favourites 'Adrian Bloom'; 'Bacchanal'; 'Bountiful'; *Dicentra cucullaria*; *D. eximia*; *D. formosa*; 'Langtrees'; 'Luxuriant'; 'Snowflakes'; *D. spectabilis*, *D. s.* 'Alba'; 'Stuart Boothman'. Plant the climbing *D. scandens* so that it can scramble through a shrub, ornamenting it with its yellow and white flowers.

Individual blooms move gently in the breeze

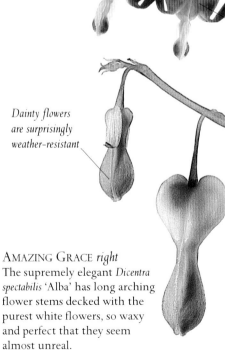

Dainty flowers are surprisingly weather-resistant

AMAZING GRACE *right*
The supremely elegant *Dicentra spectabilis* 'Alba' has long arching flower stems decked with the purest white flowers, so waxy and perfect that they seem almost unreal.

CRIMSON SHADES
'Bacchanal' is ideal for naturalizing under shrubs, where it will form attractive spreading clumps with dusky crimson flowers from mid- to late spring.

SPRING ROMANCE *above*
With its pretty pendent flowers and delicate bluish-green divided foliage, *Dicentra spectabilis* makes a handsome addition to an informal border in spring and early summer.

Dicentra spectabilis starts to flower early, so bear this in mind when planning. Choose a site sheltered from any spring frosts or strong winds to avoid damage to young growth.

Dicentras don't like being moved because they have small, fragile roots that fracture readily, so disturb them only when necessary.

◀ FLOWER SIZE
2.5cm (1in)
across

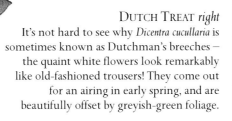

DUTCH TREAT *right*
It's not hard to see why *Dicentra cucullaria* is sometimes known as Dutchman's breeches – the quaint white flowers look remarkably like old-fashioned trousers! They come out for an airing in early spring, and are beautifully offset by greyish-green foliage.

Fritillaries *FRITILLARIA*

LATE SPRING SEES the arrival of fritillaries, their delicate flowers nodding in the slightest breeze. The first time I saw wild fritillaries was in an alpine meadow in Austria, their dainty heads almost hidden amongst the grass. It is easy to re-create this effect in the garden, with bulbs planted in miniature drifts or allowed to naturalize in grass. Use them to enhance a grassy bank or, if shade-tolerant, as unusual underplanting below trees. Fritillaries also make a wonderful display in pots or raised beds, where their flowers are brought closer to the eye for inspection – use very gritty compost in containers.

Lantern-shaped flowers are ornately patterned

CHEQUERED BEAUTY
Often known as snakeshead fritillary, *Fritillaria meleagris* has subtly chequered flowers. It is one of the most widely available fritillaries.

◀ FLOWER SIZE
4.5cm (1¾in) long

Long, slender stems support the nodding flowers

IN THE SHADE
Clusters of greeny-cream flowers are borne by *Fritillaria pallidiflora*, an excellent choice for lightening up a dull corner.

DEEP AND DUSKY
Bring a touch of glamour to the border with the regal, elegant flowers of *Fritillaria camschatcensis* in rich, deep purple.

BELLS FOR SPRING
The bell-shaped flowers of *Fritillaria acmopetala* hang on drooping stems where they nod with the slightest breeze.

GROWING FRITILLARIES

PLANT PROFILE
Hardy bulbs that will flower each year.
- SIZE Most 25–45cm (10–18in); *Fritillaria imperialis* may reach 1.5m (5ft).
- FLOWER COLOURS Red, orange, yellow, purple, lilac, pink, white, cream, brown.
- FLOWERING Mid- to late spring.
- SITE Free-draining but moist soil, in sun or part shade.

Planting Planting depths will vary depending on bulb size, but 10cm (4in) is usual. The bulbs do not store well, so buy them as soon as they become available and plant straight away. They dislike too moist a soil, particularly once flowering is over, so incorporate plenty of grit at planting. Try growing them towards the edges of shrubs so that they can benefit from the protection that the shrub provides, but not so close that they will be swamped by it.

Dividing If clumps become very congested, lift and separate offsets in autumn.

Firm fixtures Fritillaries don't like being moved, so if they are being swamped by a nearby shrub it is better to prune the shrub, if you can, than risk moving them. If you must move them, do so when the foliage has died back and try to take plenty of soil too.

Naturalizing Gently scatter the bulbs over the grass and plant them where they fall to produce a random, natural look. Move only those that are actually touching. After flowering, leave the foliage to die back naturally (which usually takes several weeks) before mowing the grass.

My favourites *Fritillaria affinis; F. camschatcensis; F. involucrata; F. meleagris alba; F. messanensis, F. m.* subsp. *gracilis; F. michailovskyi; F. pallidiflora; F. pontica; F. pyrenaica.* For naturalizing, in damp soil *F. uva-vulpis* is excellent; choose *F. meleagris* in drier areas. Try growing *F. meleagris* below deciduous shrubs such as berberis, acer or cornus, or add them to a carpet of primroses, cowslips and bluebells. They also look stunning combined with small yellow tulips, or *Anemone nemorosa* and *A. blanda.* I've grown them successfully in pots using gritty compost under "permanent" plants such as shrubs.

Central cluster of
chunky stamens

Petals have an unusual
waxy sheen

MEADOW SWEET
There is no more lovely sight
in spring than natural drifts of
fritillaries growing in rough
grass. As with any meadow-style
planting, you must leave the
grass uncut so that the leaves
can nourish the bulbs before
dying down.

FLOWER SIZE ▶
2cm (¾in)
across

Leaves are sturdy and
spear-shaped

RARE CHARMER
Still showing slight chequering, the brownish-
purple waxy flowers of *Fritillaria michailovskyi* have a
contrasting yellow rim. Very different from the
shyer but hardier snakeshead fritillaries, they
need protection in very cold winters.

*When naturalizing bulbs in a
small area, you can use a bulb
planter, but it is often easier to
lift pieces of turf carefully,
fork over the soil, add fertilizer
and then plant the bulbs about
10cm (4in) deep before
replacing the turf and watering
in well. Make sure that you
scatter the bulbs to create a
random pattern — no neat lines!*

Nicotianas NICOTIANA

BEING A PARTICULAR FAN of scented flowers, I take special delight in those varieties of nicotiana that emit their pervasive fragrance as dusk falls and colour drains from the garden. These half-hardy annuals are some of the easiest flowers to grow, and they are well suited to life in a border or in a container. They perform equally well in sun or part shade, usually flowering solidly throughout summer and into the autumn. The plants are sturdy and very tolerant of most weather extremes; they soon recover if set back by cold or battered by rain.

FRAGRANT FANFARE *left*
The elegant *Nicotiana alata* has long, trumpet-shaped flowers held on long stems, but it is their perfume that is their real charm.

SALMON SUPREME *above*
Clothed in pink as a child, I sulked all day, but I'd happily dress up my garden with Domino Series 'Salmon Pink'. Try it crammed into pots for a spectacular effect.

GROWING NICOTIANAS

PLANT PROFILE

Grown as half-hardy annuals.

- SIZE Most 25–35cm (10–14in); *Nicotiana alata* and *N. sylvestris* grow to 1.5m (5ft).
- FLOWER COLOURS Red, yellow, green, purple, lilac, pink, white, cream.
- FLOWERING Throughout the summer.
- SITE Prefer moist, well-fed soil, but grow almost anywhere, in full sun or part shade.

Sowing seeds With a greenhouse or heated propagator it's very easy to grow nicotianas from seed. Sow in early spring and plant out in late spring, after any danger of late frosts.

Containers Tubs, pots and windowboxes look wonderful crammed full of nicotianas, and if you choose the scented ones for containers near open windows, you can enjoy their perfume inside too.

Growing tip The stems and leaves of these plants usually have an unpleasant, almost sticky texture, which is perfectly natural.

Hardiness In cool climates, it is possible to maintain plants from year to year if you cut them back and cover them with a deep mulch before the first autumn frosts, but this is not always reliable, and not really worthwhile when raising new plants is so easy.

My favourites Domino Series 'Salmon Pink', *Nicotiana alata grandiflora*, 'Fragrant Cloud', 'Havana' mix, 'Havana Appleblossom', 'Lime Green'. For strong perfume, try *N. alata*, Domino Mixed, Sensation Mixed, *N. sylvestris* or the dwarf 'White Bedder'.

Generally nicotianas are best grown in groups or drifts, but the tall Nicotiana sylvestris, which forms fragrant candelabras of pure white flowers, makes so much impact that it works well grown singly in amongst other flowers in a border. The flowers close up in hot sunshine, but open again to release their heady scent in the evening.

LEMON AND LIME
Like so many other annuals, nicotianas make excellent gap fillers in amongst other plants. Here, *Nicotiana* 'Lime Green' (*also below*) adds a tangy twist to a planting of golden marguerites (*Anthemis tinctoria*). Some of the newer nicotiana varieties come in really unusual shades – great for experimenting with wacky colour combinations.

STATELY STEMS
Larger than life, *Nicotiana sylvestris* stands head and shoulders above most other nicotianas and has one of the strongest perfumes.

Central crease
on each petal

FLOWER SIZE ▷
3.5cm (1½in)
across

GRABBING THE LIMELIGHT *right*
It took me several seasons before I grew to like this extraordinary variety 'Lime Green', but now I admire its unusual colour, which, magically, appears to glow as dusk draws in.

Stems, leaves
and buds are
sticky

Daffodils *Narcissus*

THE BRIGHT, DANCING heads of daffodils are one of the most welcome sights of spring. They are available in so many different colours and sizes that it is almost impossible not to find at least one that you'd like to grow. Planting fresh bulbs each year guarantees massed colour in spring bedding and containers – or let them flower more informally year after year in the border, or naturalized in grass. But wherever you use them, plant them in groups – there's no lonelier sight than a solitary daff battling with a spring gale!

FLOWER SIZE ▶
12cm (5in)
across

SMALL PLEASURES
Grow miniature daffodils such as 'Minnow' in more exposed sites where wind might snap taller stems.

SPRING GOLD
Grown in amongst the pinky-purple flowers and attractively spotted leaves of pulmonarias and star-like purple anemones, the classic yellow flowers of 'February Gold' bring a warm, sunny glow to the whole garden in early spring. These medium-sized daffodils are particularly well suited to growing among fairly small perennials.

TRUMPET CALL
Like all full-sized daffodils, 'Bravoure' has one drawback – the dying foliage looks messy. Amongst herbaceous perennials it is soon hidden, though.

GROWING DAFFODILS

PLANT PROFILE

Hardy bulbs that flower every year.

- SIZE Most 15–50cm (6–20in); dwarf types can be as tiny as 7.5cm (3in) tall.
- FLOWER COLOURS Yellow, orange, white, cream, pink.
- FLOWERING Late winter to mid-spring.
- SITE Fertile and reasonably moisture-retentive soil, in full sun or dappled shade.

Planting Plant in autumn at a depth equal to three times the height of the bulb.

Dividing Divide congested clumps of bulbs as necessary (usually every three or four years).

Care Water regularly during dry weather, feed in spring and summer, and divide established clumps.

After flowering Remove flowers as soon they are over, but leave foliage untouched for at least six weeks after the flowers have faded to ensure healthy flowering next year.

Poor flowering If daffodils become "blind" (produce healthy leaves but few or no flowers), divide and replant, then feed regularly with foliar feed and a granular fertilizer throughout the growing period.

My favourites 'Actaea', 'Baby Moon', 'Barrett Browning', 'Bravoure', *Narcissus bulbocodium*, 'Canaliculatus', *N. cyclamineus*, 'February Silver', 'Geranium', 'Golden Bells', 'Hawera', 'Ice Wings', 'Jack Snipe', 'Martinette', 'Minnow', 'Mount Hood', *N. poeticus* var. *recurvus*, 'Sweet Charity', 'Tête-à-tête', 'Thalia'.

If you plant bulbs in slatted pond baskets, you can lift the lot after flowering to let the foliage die back elsewhere.

SIMPLE CHARMS

Surrounding its bright yellow trumpet, the brushed-back petals of 'Jack Snipe' have a windswept charm.

ALPINE FAVOURITE

For a miniature alpine-style planting, one of my favourites is *Narcissus bulbocodium*, the hoop-petticoat daffodil.

SWEET SMELL OF SUCCESS

I adore 'Geranium' for its strong, sweet perfume. The real bonus is that each flower stem bears up to six blooms.

A DAINTY DISH

The yellow cup-like trumpets of 'Canaliculatus' form prominent centrepieces for a ruff of delicate pure white petals.

OLD FAVOURITE

It is easy to create your own host of golden daffodils by planting up a drift of 'Carlton', the classic rich yellow daffodil.

FRILLS AND FLOUNCES

One of the taller daffodils, 'Mount Hood' produces creamy-white flowers with flaring, frilly-edged trumpets in mid-spring.

POET'S CORNER

A particular favourite of mine, 'Barrett Browning' has golden-yellow trumpets edged with a delicate, bright orange frill.

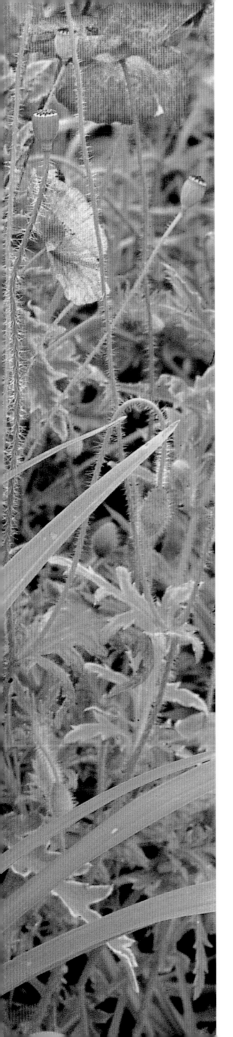

Flowers with faces

THERE ARE SOME FLOWERS THAT ARE
SO EXPRESSIVE THAT THEY GIVE A WHOLE NEW
MEANING TO THE TERM "COMPANION PLANTING".
THERE'S A FRIENDLY FLOWER WITH A FACE THAT'S
just right for almost every situation: clematis to peer
down at you from trellises and arches, pretty
herbaceous geraniums to invite you into a shady
position, and sweet-faced rock roses and jaunty
poppies tempting you over to a sunny corner. But
without a doubt, the violets and pansies – among the
best-known and best-loved flowers of all time –
present the widest range of expressions, from wide-
eyed innocence through
to a broad grin and even
a grumpy scowl. Grow
a few of my favourites
here, and there will
always be bright faces to
to say hello to whenever
you go into the garden –
and unlike your family
and neighbours, they
won't answer back!

*"Flamboyant
flowers as fine as
tissue paper
guarantee poppies
an entrée into the
best flower
borders."*

POPPIES, PAGES 110–11

Left POPPIES (PP.110–11), IRRESISTIBLE IN THEIR SIMPLICITY AND ELEGANCE

Spring anemones *ANEMONE*

PERSONALITY-WISE, anemones fall into two distinct camps. Some, such as *Anemone blanda*, are the picture of fresh, daisy-faced innocence, while others, notably *A. coronaria*, are sultry, brazen beauties in rich, solid colours. Most of the spring-flowering anemones grow from knobbly tubers or have swollen, fleshy type of roots known as rhizomes. Plant them in groups or miniature drifts – they look distinctly sad when planted singly.

GROWING ANEMONES

PLANT PROFILE

Hardy perennials.

- SIZE Most 15–30cm (6–12in).
- FLOWER COLOURS Red, blue, purple, lilac, pink, white, cream.
- FLOWERING Most early to mid-spring.
- SITE Well-drained soil, in sun or part shade. *A. nemorosa* and *A. ranunculoides* prefer shade; varieties of *A. × fulgens* and *A. coronaria* full sun.

Planting tubers Don't be put off by the shrivelled appearance of anemone tubers – despite their miserable appearance, they will produce plants! Before planting, soak the tubers first in warm (not hot) water for a few hours, perhaps overnight. They will swell up and a much higher percentage will go on to produce good, sturdy plants. Never leave tubers to soak for more than 24 hours, and be ready to plant them out as soon as you remove them from the water. Plant them about 4–5cm (1½–2in) deep.

Dividing Separate offsets from tubers or divide rhizomatous clumps in late summer or early autumn.

Naturalizing The woodland anemones *A. blanda* and *A. nemorosa* are perfect for naturalizing beneath shrubs and trees. Plant in a random fashion and leave them to spread.

My favourites *Anemone blanda* 'Ingramii', *A. b.* Radar', *A. b.* 'White Splendour'; *A. coronaria* De Caen Group 'Mister Fokker' and 'The Bride', *A. c.* St Brigid Group 'Lord Lieutenant'; *A. × fulgens*; *A. nemorosa*, *A. n.* 'Allenii', *A. n.* 'Robinsoniana; *A. ranunculoides*; *A. rivularis*. For excellent cut flowers, try *A. coronaria* De Caen and St Brigid Groups.

DARK-EYED BEAUTIES
The De Caen and St Brigid groups are full of varieties in jewel-like colours; they make superb cut flowers.

◀ FLOWER SIZE
8cm (3 ¼in)
across

Anemone nemorosa is easy to naturalize under shrubs or trees, but you must avoid mowing off the foliage, so choose areas of sparse grass or woodland-style areas.

For anemone flowers later in the year, grow the tall, clump-forming herbaceous perennials known as Japanese anemones (see pp.156–7), which flower from the end of the summer until mid-autumn.

SAFE HAVEN
Grow *Anemone coronaria* in a sheltered spot and the display will last for several weeks in spring. Avoid watering it during the summer.

WEDDING BELLE
The inner petals of *Anemone coronaria* De Caen Group 'The Bride' are subtly tinged with pale lime green towards a yellowy-green centre.

LOOKING GOOD
Although quite small, each bright magenta flower of *Anemone blanda* 'Radar' has a central white "eye" that seems to stare right back at you.

Poppies *PAPAVER*

FLAMBOYANT FLOWERS as fine as tissue paper guarantee poppies an entrée into the best flower borders. Although each bloom is short-lived, they are produced in such quantity during the summer that they create constant colour. The simple "field" poppies are annuals or are best grown as such; they are easy to raise from seed and to look after as long as they are given a sunny site. The lusher, frilly Oriental poppies are forms of *Papaver orientale*, a perennial, and will return year after year.

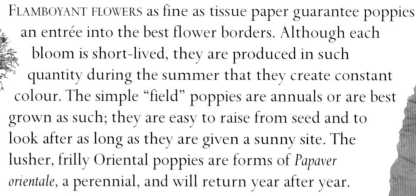

BRIGHT AND BUBBLY
Icelandic poppies, like *Papaver nudicaule* 'Champagne Bubbles' here, usually come in a mixture of yellow and oranges and are sometimes scented.

ATTRACTION OF OPPOSITES
The stark contrast between the crimson-black centre and the papery white petals of *Papaver orientale* 'Black and White' creates a minimalist impact: these are truly monochrome flowers.

DELICATE PINKS
The pink petals of *Papaver orientale* 'Cedric Morris' look as fragile and light as a puff of air, set against grey-green foliage. All varieties of *P. orientale* can be divided as soon as flowering is over.

SPELLBOUND
It's no wonder that *Papaver rhoeas* 'Mother of Pearl' is also known as 'Fairy Wings', for this relative of the corn poppy has a fairy-like quality. They are easily raised from seed, and will often self-seed.

GROWING POPPIES

PLANT PROFILE

Annuals and perennials; some short-lived perennials are best grown as annuals.

- SIZE Most 45–90cm (18–36in).
- FLOWER COLOURS Red, orange, yellow, purple, pink, white.
- FLOWERING Throughout summer.
- SITE Well-drained soil, in full sun.

Planting Perennial poppies perform well mulched with garden compost on planting and each spring.

Sowing seeds Raise perennials from seed sown in pots in a cold frame towards the end of autumn or in early spring. Annual poppies are almost impossible to transplant and, with the exception of *Papaver nudicaule*, they simply die if you attempt it, so always sow seed as thinly as possible directly in the flowering site.

Self-seeding Poppies are prolific self-seeding plants, so look out for seedlings close to parent plants and try to keep a few, even if they are not in the "ideal" place.

Flower care Regular deadheading as soon as the flowers drop their petals prolongs the flowering period.

My favourites Annuals: *Papaver commutatum* 'Ladybird', *P. rhoeas*, *P. somniferum*.
Short-lived perennials and annuals: *P. nudicaule* 'Champagne Bubbles', *P. n.* 'Red Sails'.
Perennials: *P. orientale*, *P. o.* 'Allegro Viva', *P. o.* 'Beauty Queen', *P. o.* 'Curlilocks', *P. o.* 'Mrs Perry', *P. o.* 'Perry's White', *P. o.* 'Picotée'.

Allow a few poppies to form seedheads, which look good on the plant and striking in dried flower arrangements.

◀ FLOWER SIZE
7.5cm (3in)
across

EASTERN PROMISE
With its scarlet-orange, cup-shaped flowers, *Papaver orientale* brightens up any sunny spot from late spring until mid-summer. Even its dark throat can't make it the slightest bit sombre!

Subtle gradations of colour banding across each petal

SCARLET AND BLACK *left*
The unmistakable petal patterning of *Papaver commutatum* 'Ladybird' resembles that of the classic Flanders poppy, found in abundance growing wild in the countryside of northern France.

IMPRESSIONISTS' DREAM *right*
Poppies are seen at their dreamiest grown in sizeable drifts. Each flower may not be long-lasting, but they are produced in such profusion throughout the summer and are so beautiful that I always try to find a space for a scattering of seeds.

Rock roses *CISTUS*

ALSO KNOWN AS SUN ROSES, rock roses are amongst the most reliable and beautiful plants to grow in hot, sunny areas where soil moisture is scarce. Each one of their delicate, papery, rose-like flowers lasts for only a single day, but they are produced in such numbers that these bushy plants still provide a long show of colour throughout the summer months. For real impact, grow several identical plants in a group. If you garden fairly close to the sea, you can still grow these fragile beauties, as in mild climates they stand up well to salt-laden winds.

STRIKE SILVER
Each individual rock rose bloom fades fast, but there are always masses of buds waiting to replace them. This is 'Silver Pink'.

FLOWER SIZE ▶
5.5cm (2¼in) across

Flower buds form in clusters, and open one by one

FLIGHT OF FANCY
The petals of many rock roses remind me of the wings of a newly emerged butterfly, crinkled like scrunched silk.

Rock roses are ideal container plants, especially in very sunny positions where other plants would soon suffer from drought.

Rock roses make excellent ground cover scrambling over dry, sunny banks. Try the low-growing Cistus × dansereaui 'Decumbens'.

Shelter rock roses from cold, biting winds.

SHOCKING PINK *right*
Cistus (here *C. × purpureus*) make lovely, loose, informal mounds, ideal for cascading over the edges of slightly raised beds.

GROWING ROCK ROSES

PLANT PROFILE

Shrubby perennials, fully hardy only in warm gardens and in protected positions; they can be badly damaged by frost.

- SIZE Most 60–120cm (2–4ft), some to 2.7m (9ft).
- FLOWER COLOURS Pink, white, often with blotches.
- FLOWERING Late spring to mid-summer.
- SITE Sandy and very free-draining soil in full sun.

Sowing seeds You can sow in spring, in a cold frame, for plants to set out the following spring. Hybrids do not breed true from saved seed.

Planting Mid- to late spring. Add extra grit to improve drainage. Rock roses resent being moved, so try to choose the right spot first time!

Cuttings Take semi-ripe, heeled cuttings, using non-flowering side shoots, 7.5–10cm (3–4in) long, in mid-summer. Root them in a heated propagator at about 16°C (61°F). Keep the young plants under cover over winter and plant out in spring.

Pruning Only prune established cistus if absolutely necessary. Once young plants have finished flowering, you can pinch them back to encourage plenty of bushy growth and to prevent them from becoming straggly. Once an older plant has become straggly, it is best discarded as it will not respond well to pruning, usually dying back further.

My favourites *Cistus × aguilarii* 'Maculatus', *C. × cyprius*, *C. × dansereaui* 'Decumbens', *C. × hybridus*, *C. incanus* subsp. *creticus*, *C. ladinifer*, *C.* 'Peggy Sammons', *C. × pulverulentus* 'Sunset', *C. × purpureus*, *C. × skanbergii*.

BIRD CALL *right*

With its contrasting crimson eye at the base of each white petal, *Cistus × dansereaui* 'Decumbens' reminds me of an exotically feathered bird. This superb low-growing shrub attracts attention all through the summer.

Hellebores *HELLEBORUS*

THE SHY, SUBTLE, BELL-LIKE FLOWERS of hellebores put them among my most treasured winter-garden plants. Choose carefully, and you can have hellebores in bloom from early winter right through until mid-spring. These moisture-loving plants will thrive in part shade, and some will even grow in full shade, brightening up the gloomiest corners of the garden. Many of these hardy perennials have robust, attractive foliage, too, bringing year-round interest to the border.

PERFECT STRANGER *above*
Hellebores hybridize so freely that their offspring may never be given "official" names. The results are often lovely, as here, and well worth growing.

FRECKLE FACE *left*
Many of the most appealing hellebores have delicately freckled petals, like this *Helleborus orientalis.*

GREEN GODDESS
The unusual green-flowered *Helleborus cyclophyllus* is one of my favourites, not least for the bonus of its delicate scent.

WHITE CHRISTMAS
The classic *Helleborus niger*, best-known as the Christmas rose, produces beautiful white flowers sometimes flushed with pink.

GROWING HELLEBORES

PLANT PROFILE

Hardy perennials.
- SIZE 45–90cm (18–36in).
- FLOWER COLOURS Green, purple, lilac, pink, white, cream, yellow; some may be freckled with contrasting colour.
- FLOWERING Throughout mid-winter to late spring.
- SITE Moist soil, in partial shade. Once established, leave them in peace as they resent root disturbance.

Soil Unless you can improve dry or thin soil so that it becomes more moisture-retentive it is not worth growing hellebores, as they will not thrive. Improve soil by incorporating well-rotted compost before planting.

Sowing seeds Saving and sowing seed from hellebores is a great way of getting interesting plants, as the offspring will not be the same as the parents, but often have lovely colours and markings. Sow ripe seed taken in early to mid-summer and plant in sandy compost in a cold frame. It will take three years before you have flowering-sized plants.

Dividing You can divide mature clumps in autumn, but keep plenty of soil around the roots.

Watering Keep hellebores well watered during dry weather.

Fantastic flowers Cut off the leaves of *H. orientalis* in late winter to really show the flowers off at their best. New leaves will grow in spring.

Leaf damage The fungal disease hellebore leafspot may do a lot of damage. Control it by picking off affected leaves and, if necessary, spray with a suitable fungicide.

My favourites *Helleborus* Ashwood Garden hybrids; *H. atrorubens*; *H. foetidus* 'Wester Flisk'; *H. lividus*; *H. niger*, *H. n.* 'Potter's Wheel'; *H. orientalis*. With its pale, almost emerald-green flowers, *H. argutifolius* looks splendid interplanted with *Iris reticulata*. *H. cyclophyllus* has the bonus of perfume from its yellowish-green flowers. *H. orientalis* is lovely planted amongst a drift of snowdrops, perhaps beneath a favourite tree or shrub. Try combining *H. foetidus* with winter-flowering heathers.

FLOWER SIZE ▶
6.5cm (2¼in)
across

MYSTERY GUEST
More proof that it pays to keep and
grow on any seedling hellebores
you may find in the garden.
Although plants may take several
years to reach flowering size,
with results like this it
is surely well worth
the wait.

*Dark purple flecks
scattered on pink-
flushed petals*

*Prominent golden
stamens are grouped
in a central cluster*

A ROSE FOR SPRING *left*
From mid-winter to mid-spring
Helleborus orientalis, the evocatively
named (if often rather premature)
Lenten Rose, produces white,
greenish-cream or almost velvety
purple-red flowers. But even before it
blooms, this clump-forming hellebore
is well worth growing for its large,
handsome, shiny green leaves.

*Hellebores make gorgeous cut
flowers, so always grow a few
extra plants just for indoor
arrangements. I recommend
Helleborus argutifolius,
H. atrorubens, H. foetidus
(don't crush the leaves, as they
give off an unpleasant smell)
and H. niger.*

*Helleborus foetidus is ideal
for very shady sites; it thrives
in such locations.*

Violets and pansies *VIOLA*

DARK MYSTERY
Amongst plant enthusiasts in particular there is often a lot of fuss and intrigue about "black" flowers – grow *Viola* 'Molly Sanderson' and you will soon understand why.

PERHAPS IT'S THEIR bright, often impish faces that make violets and pansies so appealing, but I'm sure that they are also popular because they are just so simple to grow. Both easy and eager to please, they'll put on a good display in most conditions, often flowering continuously all summer. If you choose winter-flowering types, they will not only perform well throughout winter and spring but carry on through summer, if given the chance. You can use versatile violas in almost any situation – baskets, windowboxes, beds, borders, for edging and in rock gardens.

VIOLET EYES
For a simple, subtle colourway, *Viola cornuta* 'Purple Duet' uses two shades of mauve to offset its contrasting bright yellow eye.

BLEND OF BLUE
Not all violas have sharply defined markings: the flowers of *Viola cornuta* 'Blueberry Cream' have beautifully graded colour.

MARKS OF DISTINCTION
above and below
Like little cat's whiskers, these striking pollen guidelines are a feature of many violets.

JEWEL BRIGHT *above*
Many pansies come in mixed colours. Here, *Viola* × *wittrockiana* Forerunner Series creates a stained-glass effect.

◀ FLOWER SIZE
2cm (¾in)
across

GROWING VIOLETS AND PANSIES

PLANT PROFILE

Annuals or perennials for summer or winter displays; they are perfectly hardy.

- SIZE 5–30cm (2–12in).
- FLOWER COLOURS Red, orange, yellow, blue, purple, lilac, pink, white, cream, brown.
- FLOWERING Throughout spring, summer and winter, depending on variety.
- SITE Ideally, well-drained soil, in slight shade.

Soil Violets and pansies grow well in almost any soil, although they prefer a well-drained spot. They will not last as long in heavy clay.

Position A slightly shaded spot is best, but they also perform well in full sun. If conditions are too gloomy, they tend to grow taller and become slightly leggy.

Sowing seeds Easy to raise from seed, and a huge selection is available. The seeds should germinate well in a cold frame in summer or in a shady part of the garden protected from birds.

Flower care Deadhead regularly to ensure a plentiful and long-lasting display of flowers. Leave one or two seedheads to develop if you want to raise a few plants from seed. If plants become straggly, give them a trim with a pair of scissors in late summer to encourage denser growth and, often, more flowers.

My favourites *Viola canina*; *V. cornuta* 'Blueberry Cream', *V. c.* 'Sorbet Blueberry Duet', *V. c.* 'Sorbet Purple Duet', *V. c.* var. *minor*; 'Molly Sanderson'; *V. tricolor*, *V. t.* 'Bowles' Black'; *V.* × *wittrockiana* Forerunner Series.

Violets and pansies are very widely available in bedding strips, ready to plant out for fast-growing colour.

Sharply contrasting blotches of colour define the "face"

TRIED AND TESTED

For either winter or summer colour, pansies – here, *Viola* × *wittrockiana* 'Turbo Red' (*above*), 'White Blotch' (*below*) and 'Violet Blotch' (*right*) – can be relied upon to put on a good display.

Central area is covered in soft down

Purple markings form the outline of a butterfly

◀ FLOWER SIZE 5cm (2in) across

Clematis *CLEMATIS*

EASY TO GROW, VERSATILE and incredibly pretty, clematis must easily be the most popular of the flowering climbers. They look terrific grown traditionally, clambering up walls and fences, but I squeeze more into the garden scrambling through trees, shrubs or other climbers – even as ground cover, to create a carpet of colour. The large-flowered types shown here flower during summer, but by choosing carefully, you can use clematis to bring vertical colour to your garden almost all year round.

BIG ATTRACTION
From late spring to early summer, the large blue-purple flowers and cream anthers of 'H. F. Young' are impossible to miss. As with other clematis that flower at a similar time, prompt deadheading encourages a second flush of flowers in late summer or early autumn.

STATE PRESENCE
Reliable and prolific, 'The President' has large, rich purple flowers in bloom from early summer until early autumn.

FADED GRANDEUR
The early-flowering 'Bees' Jubilee' prefers partial shade. The flower colour fades with age, or if grown in too sunny a position.

ABOUT TOWN
To avoid leaf scorch, grow 'Ville de Lyon' through an evergreen shrub. Bright carmine flowers appear in mid- to late summer.

GROWING CLEMATIS

PLANT PROFILE

Hardy perennials.

- SIZE Most 2.4–6m (8–20ft)
- FLOWER COLOURS Red, yellow, blue, purple, lilac, pink, white, cream.
- FLOWERING Most spring to late summer, depending on type.
- SITE Position in sun or part shade, always with the base of the plant in shade. A neutral loamy soil is ideal, but they can do well in lime and chalk.

Planting Set the crown of the plant 10–15cm (4–6in) beneath the soil surface. Keep the roots cool by deep planting and by covering the soil around the root area with decorative stones or slabs.

Cuttings Take semi-ripe cuttings in mid-summer, 10–12cm (4–5in) long, with at least two buds at the base. To root, they need a heated propagator set at 15–18°C (59–64°F).

Pruning Varies greatly. You only need prune *C. montana* and other small-flowered spring clematis if they become too big. For large-flowered hybrids flowering in late spring/early summer, prune lightly after flowering, removing weak and dead wood and cutting stems back to healthy buds. Prune clematis that flower later in summer and in autumn by cutting hard back to about 25cm (10in) of ground level in late winter or early spring.

My favourites *Clematis alpina* 'Pink Flamingo', *C. a.* 'Ruby'; *C. armandii*; 'Blue Belle'; *C. cirrhosa* 'Freckles'; *C. florida* 'Sieboldii'; 'Gypsy Queen'; 'Hagley Hybrid'; 'Henryi'; 'Marie Boisselot'; *C. montana* 'Elizabeth', *C. m.* var. *rubens*; 'Nelly Moser'; 'Niobe'.

Clematis look at their most natural when allowed to scramble through a tree, shrub or hedge, and can add an extra season of interest to their host plant. Initially, train the stems towards the trunk on canes or trellis, then allow the clematis to do as it pleases.

*Twining leaf-
stalks readily
attach to
support*

FLOWER SIZE ▶
7.5–10cm (3–4in)
across

PRETTY MISS *above*
Beautiful, glossy white
flowers cover 'Miss Bateman' in
early summer; like many of the large-
flowered hybrids, she often produces a
second flush in early autumn.

PROTECTIVE CAMOUFLAGE *left*
As clematis age, they often become
bare around the base, but planting a
small shrub in front disguises this
shortcoming, and also gives the roots
some shade – which clematis need –
in sunny spots.

Geraniums *GERANIUM*

WITH THEIR SIMPLE, unostentatious beauty, herbaceous geraniums always look, to me, a little surprised by their recent surge in popularity. But in my view, few plants work harder to deserve it more: there are geraniums that will be "good doers" for almost any site; they get on well with, and usually flatter, most other garden plants; and they flower their little hearts out for months and months. What is more, the foliage is pretty, and in many develops lovely autumnal tints as the seasons change; be sure to position these where you can enjoy the turning colours.

Faded flowers resemble the head of a crane, hence "cranesbill"

IN A DISTINCTIVE VEIN
The pale purply-pink flowers of 'Salome' are given character by the dark purple markings etched on the almost luminous petals, offset by pale green leaves.

TRICK OF THE LIGHT
The pure purple petals of *Geranium himalayense* 'Gravetye' form simple discs of colour which seem to light up when the sun is behind them: fantastic next to yellow flowers.

SHADES OF SUMMER
A pretty plant for a shady spot, *Geranium phaeum* has petals so delicate that they could have been cut from finest silk. In contrast, the prominent stamens shout out for attention.

SILVERY STUNNERS
White-flowered varieties such as this *Geranium phaeum* 'Album' look stunning surrounded by the silvery-white variegated foliage of *Lamium maculatum* 'Beacon Silver' or 'White Nancy'.

PERFECT PARTNERS
Plant violet-flowered geraniums under a pink rose – here, *Geranium × magnificum* with *Rosa* 'Fantin-Latour'. Roses often develop bare lower stems, which the geraniums will hide.

GROWING GERANIUMS

PLANT PROFILE

Hardy perennials.

- SIZE 15–105cm (6–42in).
- FLOWER COLOURS White, pink, purple, lilac, blue.
- FLOWERING Early summer to late autumn.
- SITE Some geraniums do well in full shade, but most prefer either sun or part shade. Unfussy about soil, except for alpine geraniums, which need good drainage.

Support Use twiggy sticks to subtly support taller varieties.

Fantastic flowers Cut back after flowering to encourage dense growth and a second flush of flowers.

Division Divide established clumps at the end of the summer or in spring.

Cuttings You can take root cuttings from *Geranium pratense* and *G. sanguineum*, as both have thick roots.

Sowing seed Species come true from seed. Sow in spring in a cold frame and plant out in autumn.

My favourites 'Ann Folkard', *Geranium cinereum* 'Ballerina', *G. gracile*, *G. × oxonianum* 'Wargrave Pink', *G. pratense* f. *albiflorum*, 'Salome', *G. sanguineum*, *G. sylvaticum* 'Album'. For edging a large border, 'Johnson's Blue' is ideal, with a compact, mound-like habit and blue flowers. *G. × oxonianum* 'Walter's Gift' and *G. phaeum* 'Samobor' have particularly attractive foliage. The magenta-purple flowers of *G. psilostemon* look fantastic with buttercups or mingling with *Rosa* 'Maigold', which gives the stems support. *G. himalayense* 'Gravetye', *G. macrorrhizum* 'Album', *G. phaeum* and *G. p.* 'Album' are good in shade.

Low-growing, compact geraniums such as Geranium clarkei 'Kashmir White' make pretty, informal edging.

Look closely to see the etched lines that guide insects towards the pollen

◀ FLOWER SIZE
3cm (1¼in)
across

REACH FOR THE SKY
The lavender-pink flowers of *Geranium maculatum* 'Chatto' light up the partly shaded sites it enjoys. Taller geraniums such as this often need staking, particularly in shade, where they usually grow more vigorously.

Stems may need support; twiggy sticks are ideal for these informal plants

PART
THREE

PERFECT PLANTING

Right plant, right place

MATCHING A PLANT TO THE conditions you can offer it makes good garden sense. Put a plant where it naturally feels at home and it is more likely to thrive, with little work from you. By slightly altering the conditions, you can of course bend the rules, for example by incorporating bulky organic matter into the soil to improve moisture retention, by adding grit to beds or planting holes to improve drainage, or by planting a leafy shrub to create shelter from sun for a shade-loving plant. If you take care, amending your site to suit a plant's needs will work, though the chances are that you will have to lavish more care on a plant growing in "artificial" surroundings than one growing in a naturally suitable site.

A GREEN AND PLEASANT PLACE
There isn't as wide a choice of flowering plants for shade as in sun, but you can cheat to enhance the effect: here, pale epimediums are boosted by the white-splashed foliage of shade-loving hostas.

GARDEN CHECKLIST

Always check the requirements of a plant against what your garden can offer before you buy. Point-of-sale material and plant labels should provide you with most of the information you need, and don't be slow to ask for advice. Points you should consider include:

1 The soil pH or acidity: some plants may discolour or even die in acid soil.

2 Sunlight needs: in dull conditions sun-loving plants will produce fewer blooms.

3 Moisture content of soil: too wet or too free-draining may cause root death.

4 Overall climate: will the plant survive your winter, or will it need shelter?

5 Open or sheltered site: in exposed areas, winds in particular may be drying.

6 The aspect: does the site face north, south? How much sun does it get in the day?

7 Planting against a wall: it may act as a suntrap, but will rain reach the plant?

8 Sloping ground: tends to be drier at the top, becoming wetter towards the base.

PLANT CHECKLIST

Having satisfied yourself that your garden or site will suit the plant you'd like to grow, don't forget to consider these two essential points:

SIZE
Check the mature size of the plant. It may look small and well behaved when you first see it, but appearances can be deceptive. Before you know it, it may grow far too big, shading or swamping other plants nearby, blocking a path or shading the lawn. It may be possible to prune the plant to keep it to the required dimensions, but some plants respond better to this than others. Pruning could ruin its natural shape or even cause it to die back.

SAFETY
Some plants are known to be potentially hazardous: they may cause poisoning, mild gastric upsets or adverse skin reactions of varying severity. The whole plant may be a risk or it may have seasonal features, such as poisonous berries, that pose a threat. If the garden is to be used by children, be especially vigilant about the plants that you choose to grow. Similarly, plants with thorns or irritant hairs may be better suited to out-of-the way places.

FINDING THE RIGHT SITE *right*

Moist soil, dappled shade and fairly humid air suit plants such as these ligularias, astilbes and mimulus down to the ground, creating a gorgeous display with little effort on your part. Plants less at home in these conditions may become drawn and leggy, fail to flower and be more prone to pests and diseases. Some plants tolerate a range of conditions: the astilbes, for instance (*also below*) will grow in boggy soil in sun, or in drier (but still moisture-retentive) soil in shade, so could be used as linking plants to create continuity between plantings in different areas of the garden.

What plant where?

TO BE HONEST, it's hard not to behave like a kid let loose in a sweetshop when you're at the garden centre. But before you succumb to love at first sight in every direction, do check that the plants that have caught your eye are suitable for your garden, especially for challenging areas – deep shade, damp, a dry spot – or you may be in for a disappointment. Turn less-than-perfect conditions to your advantage by choosing plants that will positively thrive, not just survive, in them.

SUNNY AND DRY
Hot sun, free-draining soil, sloping ground and even windy conditions can all create a dry site. These *Gazania* 'Orange Beauty' positively thrive in a dry soil and love basking in the sun.

MOVEABLE FEAST *above*
If your garden has mostly hard surfaces, or you simply want "instant colour", plants in containers are the answer. Here, begonias add seasonal colour.

SOIL SOLUTIONS *right*
Many people worry about having alkaline soil, but there are plenty of smashing plants that thrive on chalk or lime. These *Physostegia virginiana* and anemones couldn't look happier.

CURTAIN CALL *above*

Boring vertical surfaces cry out for a climber or wall shrub. Here, the richly perfumed blooms of honeysuckle clamber around a window so its perfume can be enjoyed both inside and out.

Corydalis flexuosa

COOL BEAUTY *left*

Shady areas need luminous colours. These blue *Corydalis flexuosa* and white dicentras really freshen up the lovely hues and textures of subtle foliage plants.

WATER WAYS *right*

A damp corner or boggy ground alongside a water feature offer the ideal conditions for lush planting. Here, swathes of the golden-yellow marsh marigold (*Caltha palustris*) are complemented by variegated iris foliage.

Plants with a purpose

WE CHOOSE PLANTS for all sorts of reasons. Often it simply comes down to pure visual appeal, and there's nothing wrong with that (as long as they'll be happy in the spot you have in mind). But wouldn't it be wonderful if that same plant also smelt divine, brought clouds of butterflies into the garden, or was ideal for cutting? The flowering plants I've chosen on the following pages aren't just for solving problem sites; they all have "added value" – the bonus of beautiful foliage, for example – to repay your care.

EASY PICKINGS *above*
What could be better than a plant that looks good in the flower border and can also be cut and used indoors in flower arrangements? These Chinese lanterns (*Physalis alkekengi* var. *franchetii*) are grown for their bright orange, bell-shaped seedheads, which look superb in dried flower displays.

DOWN TO EARTH *left*
Bare earth has little appeal and usually attracts weeds in no time, making it both uninteresting and hard work. Using ground-cover plants can transform such a patch into a carpet of colour and texture. Here, the rosette-forming *Tiarella cordifolia* combines pretty flowers with attractive, dense foliage.

GREEN DREAM *above*
Most plants are in leaf for a much greater proportion of the year than they are in flower, so anything that has distinctive foliage is of interest. The flowers of *Alchemilla mollis* are incredibly pretty, but the greyish-green, geometrically shaped leaves are so gorgeous that it would be worth using even if it never flowered.

BUTTERFLY BALL *above and left*
No garden is complete without its quota of busy, friendly insects. Above, a small tortoiseshell butterfly briefly feeds on a sedum. Many flowers attract beneficial insects. These *Monarda didyma* 'Cambridge Scarlet' (*left*) with their crazy mop-head flowers and dazzling colour not only brighten up a late summer border; as far as butterflies and bees are concerned, someone has kindly laid on a feast of nectar.

FLOWER FILLERS *above*
Quick-growing annuals that are easily raised from seed are an excellent way to fill gaps in new or established plantings. Here, masses of pink *Lavatera trimestris* add to the glorious but more subtle colours of nearby *Anemone × hybrida* and a pale pink rose.

SCENT TO PLEASE
Thymes are excellent value: these tough little plants soften path edges, and actually reward the odd careless footfall with a burst of aromatic fragrance from their crushed leaves. Here they spread themselves invitingly before a garden bench backed by cool blue catmints.

Scented flowers

FOR ME, A GARDEN isn't complete unless it includes plenty of scented flowers and aromatic foliage. The combination of flowers, foliage and perfume is a heady cocktail, and by choosing carefully you can even enjoy scent in the evening as well as in the day – heaven!

OTHER FLOWERS FOR SCENT

Wallflowers (*Cheiranthus cheiri*) pp.154–5	Honeysuckle (*Lonicera*) pp.134–5
Sweet peas (*Lathyrus odoratus*) pp.56–7	Daffodils (*Narcissus*) pp.104–5
Lilies (*Lilium*) pp.62–3	Nicotiana (*Nicotiana*) pp.102–3

SWEET NATURED
Forming a neat mound, *Heliotropium arborescens* 'Marine', like other heliotropes, brings rich colour and a gorgeous perfume into the garden in summer.

BELLES OF THE BORDER
Stocks may come in widely different shapes, sizes and colours – here, the compact *Matthiola incana* Cinderella Series – but all of them have a strong, rich scent.

PLANT	SIZE	APPEARANCE
LILY-OF-THE-VALLEY *Convallaria majalis*	H 15–20cm (6–8in) S 15cm (6in)	From mid- to late spring this hardy perennial spreads rapidly to create a fragrant carpet of arching flower stems draped with tiny bell-like flowers in white or pale pink.
BURNING BUSH *Dictamnus albus*	H 65cm (26in) S 25cm (10in)	Summer and a tang of citrus go together, so find a sunny spot for this hardy herbaceous perennial with its lemon-scented foliage and flowers. Striking spikes of star-shaped white flowers appear in early summer.
FREESIAS *Freesia*	H 30–45cm (12–18in) S 7.5–10cm (3–4in)	Giving off a sweet, warm and spicy scent, the delicate sprays of funnel-shaped flowers, in white or shades of lilac, purple, red, yellow, cream or pink, are a definite hit in late spring and early summer.
HELIOTROPE *Heliotropium arborescens*	H 45–60cm (18–24in) S 20–25cm (8–10in)	Perfect for patio containers, the flowers, in white or shades of purple, violet or blue, have a delightful perfume and are packed into dense heads throughout the summer. Best grown as a half-hardy annual.
SWEET ROCKET *Hesperis matronalis*	H 90cm (3ft) S 30cm (12in)	Sweet rocket has pink, white or purple fragrant flower spikes that appear in early and mid-summer. Its fragrance, while good in the day, is sublime once the sun goes down.
HYACINTHS *Hyacinthus*	H 20–25cm (8–10in) S 10–15cm (4–6in)	You either love or hate the overpowering scent of hyacinths. The dense flower spikes packed with horizontal, bell-shaped flowers in white or shades of pink, blue, yellow or cream are spring classics.
STOCKS *Matthiola*	H 30–50cm (12–20in) S 30cm (12in)	Dense, blowzy, sweet-scented flower spikes develop from late spring to mid-summer. Flowers may be single, double or a mixture of both on one spike and come in white or shades of pink, lilac or mauve.
EVENING PRIMROSE *Oenothera biennis*	H 90cm (3ft) S 40cm (16in)	The fragrant, fragile-looking yellow flowers of this hardy biennial bloom from early summer until the middle of autumn. Most open as the sun sets – perfect by a terrace where you sit or eat in the evenings.
HERBACEOUS BORDER PHLOX *Phlox paniculata*	H 30–90cm (12–36in) S 90cm (3ft)	An essential ingredient of any herbaceous border in late summer, the showy pink, red, lilac, bluish-mauve or white flowerheads, up to 15cm (6in) across, produce a very sweet fragrance that seems to hang in the air.
THYMES *Thymus*	H 5–25cm (2–10in) S 15–45cm (6–18in)	The pungent, aromatic foliage of these creeping evergreen perennials is topped with tiny white, pink or purple flowers in mid-summer. Some forms have attractively variegated or woolly foliage.

Sheer strength of perfume is combined here with the intensely purplish-blue flowerheads of *Hyacinthus orientalis* 'Blue Jacket'.

SITE	CULTIVATION	HINTS AND TIPS
A site in dappled shade or in full sun; soil must be moist.	Plant crowns in autumn or early spring, just beneath the surface. Mulch regularly with leafmould to keep the soil moist. Divide established plants in winter.	• For pale pink flowers, choose *C. majalis* var. *rosea*. • For superb variegated creamy-white and green-striped foliage, choose 'Albostriata'. The leaves make a lovely surround for the flowers in a tiny vase or posy.
A sunny site with free-draining, ideally alkaline soil.	Plant container-grown plants at any time of year in a spot where you can enjoy their aroma. It resents disturbance, so avoid moving once established.	• *D. albus* var. *purpureus* has scented mauve flowers streaked with purple. • The volatile oil produced by the flowers and leaves may occasionally cause skin irritation. • Use the starry seedheads in dried arrangements.
Well-drained soil, in a sheltered, sunny spot.	Freesias can't survive winter cold. Plant corms about 3cm (1¼in) deep, ideally in early spring. Lift in autumn, and store in a dry, cool, but frost-free place.	• If necessary, when planting incorporate grit to improve drainage. Provide twiggy sticks for support in windy areas. • In cold-winter areas, make a diary note for an autumn weekend to remind you to lift the corms.
Well-drained soil, in full sun.	Sow seeds in late winter at 16–18°C (61–64°F) or buy as small plants. Plant out after any late frosts. Take under cover or discard at the end of summer.	• Choose the dwarf 'Marine' for plants with rich purple flowers that grow only 30cm (12in) high. • Overwinter heliotropes in a cool, frost-free porch or greenhouse. Trim lightly in spring. • Heliotropes thrive in containers.
Thrives on a poor soil and loves some shade.	Best grown as a hardy annual or short-lived perennial. Sweet rocket prefers a well-drained soil, so incorporate leafmould or garden compost when planting.	• Replace plants every two or three years or grow as an annual. • Divide established plants in spring or take basal cuttings in late spring or early summer. Only the species can be grown from seed.
Best in a well-drained soil, in sun.	Plant the bulbs in containers or borders between late summer and late autumn. Plant 10cm (4in) deep and 15–20cm (6–8in) apart. Hyacinths are hardy.	• After their first year, the bulbs tend to produce only weak, sparsely covered flower spikes. Ideally, buy new bulbs each year. • Aphids and slugs may be a problem, so control these pests if necessary.
Well-fed, moist soil, in sun or part shade.	Available as young plants, or sow seed direct outside in mid-spring (half-hardy annuals) or early/mid-summer and then overwinter (half-hardy biennials).	• Taller varieties may need some support as they can become top-heavy. • For quick results, choose *M. incana* 'Seven Week' or 'Ten Week', which should flower in about the stated number of weeks after the seed is sown.
Needs plenty of sun and well-drained, preferably sandy soil.	Best planted in either autumn or spring and kept well-watered during spring and summer. If growing from seed, sow direct in spring.	• Plants may tend to flop, so subtle staking with canes or pea sticks is often necessary. • A rampant self-seeder – once planted in the garden be prepared to weed out numerous seedlings, or it may become invasive.
A sunny or part-shaded site, in well-fed, moisture-retentive soil.	Plant in autumn or spring, incorporating extra organic matter. Every three or four years divide established clumps and replant on a fresh site.	• Powdery mildew disease is a common and damaging problem, especially towards the end of the summer on plants that have got too dry. • 'White Admiral' and 'Starfire' are my particular favourites, great for attracting bees and butterflies.
Free-draining soil, in a very sunny, sheltered spot.	Plant in very early summer or in spring. Replace plants every few years, as they become straggly. After flowering, give a gentle "hair cut" to keep plants dense.	• Thymes are perfect for growing in cracks and crevices in paving, around steps or on a terrace. • Interesting varieties are *T.* × *citriodorus* (lemon thyme), 'Aureus' (variegated yellow foliage) and 'Silver Queen' (variegated cream and white).

Delicate, starry flowers are carried in compact spikes by *Dictamnus albus* var. *purpureus*, forming a scented, pinky-white haze above the plant.

Freesia is the one scented flower I cannot be without, in the garden or in the home. The combination of its graceful shape, rich yet delicate colours and fantastic fragrance is irresistible.

Fast-growing flowers

THE PLANTS HERE are ideal for filling the odd unexpected gap or for making a new border or garden quickly seem more established. Not only will the garden soon look better, but you will also feel that you have really achieved something in a relatively short space of time.

OTHER FAST-GROWING FLOWERS

Clematis (*Clematis*) pp.118–19
Cobaea scandens pp.134–5
Eryngiums (*Eryngium*) pp.68–9

Geraniums (*Geranium*) pp.120–1
Morning glory (*Ipomoea*) pp.134–5
Sweet peas (*Lathyrus odoratus*) pp.56–7

QUICK FIX *above*
In no time at all, *Crambe cordifolia* produces statuesque stems, ideal for gaps at the back of the flower border.

FAST WORKER *left*
The vigorous *Prunella grandiflora* soon covers the ground and by summer is topped with whorls of rich purple flowers.

PLANT	SIZE	APPEARANCE
CANNA LILIES *Canna* × *generalis* hybrids	H 60–80cm (24–32in) S 45cm (18in)	The combination of large, flamboyant leaves and trumpet-shaped flowers in brilliant shades of red, orange or yellow make cannas real attention-grabbers. Half-hardy, they flower from mid-summer.
SPIDER FLOWER *Cleome hassleriana*	H 1.2m (4ft) S 45cm (18in)	If you grow it from seed, this half-hardy annual is great value, with striking, spidery pink, white or purple scented flowers on towering stems from early summer through until early autumn.
CRAMBE *Crambe cordifolia*	H 2.4m (8ft) S 1.5m (5ft)	This superb, unusually tall herbaceous perennial is covered in masses of tiny, star-shaped white flowers in early summer creating a pretty, cloud-like haze with a sweet perfume.
DIASCIAS *Diascia*	H 45cm (18in) S 40cm (16in)	These herbaceous perennials bear large numbers of delicate pink, peachy or near-red flowers in loose spikes throughout the summer and into early autumn. They are not reliably hardy.
PERENNIAL PEA *Lathyrus latifolius*	H 3m (10ft) S 90cm (3ft)	A very fast-growing and vigorous hardy herbaceous climber that soon clambers up a trellis or through shrubs. Flowers are not scented but come in white or lovely shades of pink or red, in summer to early autumn.
LOOSESTRIFE *Lythrum salicaria*	H 1.2m (4ft) S 45cm (18in)	This is a real hit with butterflies and bees! In mid-summer plants are smothered in dense spikes of flowers in shades of pink. *L. salicaria* and its varieties reliably bring splashes of colour to boggy ground.
SOLOMON'S SEAL *Polygonatum odoratum*	H 60cm (2ft) S 30cm (12in)	Any shady spot can be given a quick lift in spring by this fragrant herbaceous perennial. The foliage is pretty, and the scented white flowers, tinged with green, hang from delicately arching stems.
SELF-HEAL *Prunella grandiflora*	H 25cm (10in) S 90cm (3ft)	Useful as ground cover, this herbaceous perennial produces violet, purple, white or pink flowers throughout the summer. The flowers develop on small spikes within a ring of showy, leafy bracts.
SISYRINCHIUM *Sisyrinchium striatum*	H 45–60cm (18–24in) S 30cm (12in)	The sword-shaped leaves of this hardy perennial, striped in the bold variety 'Variegatum', are held in fans. Cream or yellowish flowers, held in spikes, appear continuously throughout the summer.
HARDY TRADESCANTIA *Tradescantia* × *andersoniana*	H 40–60cm (16–24in) S 45cm (18in)	A pretty, clump-forming, hardy herbaceous perennial, which produces a succession of three-petalled flowers from early summer to early autumn. Depending on the variety flower colour is blue, purple, pink or lilac.

SITE	CULTIVATION	HINTS AND TIPS
Cannas need well-drained soil and plenty of sun.	Plant in spring, after the last frosts are over. In autumn, lift the fleshy roots, remove dead areas and store in moist sawdust in a cool, frost-free place.	• If you have a cool greenhouse you can plant stored roots in individual pots of compost/sand mix in very early spring to start them into growth early. • My favourites are 'Wyoming', 'Black Knight' and 'Rosemond Coles'.
Likes well-drained, sandy soil in sun.	Sow seed in a heated greenhouse or heated propagator in early spring. Plant out as soon as any late frosts are over in late spring or early summer.	• Remove faded blooms regularly to increase the number of flowers produced. • Striking varieties include 'Helen Campbell', 'Violet Queen', 'Pink Queen' and 'Cherry Queen'. • Spider flowers thrive in containers.
A sunny site with well-drained soil. Will thrive even on poor soil.	Plant in autumn or early spring. Divide established plants in late spring. Sow seed in spring in a heated propagator, pot on, then plant out when large enough.	• Crambe is an ideal plant for the back of the border, providing a good textural backdrop for all sorts of colour schemes. • Crambe dies back shortly after flowering, so plant up the gap left with late-flowering annuals.
Well-drained but moist soil, in sun or part shade.	Best planted in spring, adding a balanced fertilizer to the soil. Divide established plants in spring or take semi-ripe cuttings in summer.	• After the first flush of flowers, cut the plants back and a second, later display should develop. • Lovely varieties include 'Lilac Belle', 'Rupert Lambert', 'Salmon Supreme', 'Blackthorn Apricot' and 'Ruby Field'.
Thrives in any reasonable soil, in sun or, preferably, part shade.	Plant in spring, and grow as ground cover or as a climber. Seed can be sown direct into the ground in early spring or in individual pots.	• Cut flowers or deadhead regularly to prevent pods forming and so prolong flowering. • Slugs can be a problem, especially if the plants are grown as ground cover. • Choose the species for purplish-pink flowers.
Moist or even boggy soil, in sun or part shade.	Plant during suitable weather between autumn and spring. Divide established clumps in autumn or spring or take semi-ripe cuttings in spring.	• Deadhead regularly to encourage flowering and reduce the number of variable self-sown seedlings. • Choose named varieties for the best-looking plants. I like 'Firecandle' (rose-pink), 'The Beacon' (even richer pink) and 'Robert' (bright pink).
Well-drained soil, in dappled shade.	Plant during suitable conditions between late autumn and early spring, adding leafmould or compost to the soil. Divide established clumps in spring.	• If plants start to lose their vigour, lift and divide them, discarding the older sections. • Plants may be attacked by Solomon's seal sawfly larvae. Pick the larvae off or spray with a suitable product.
Either a sunny or partly shaded site. Self-heal grows well in almost all soils.	Best planted in early spring, self-heal is very easy to grow and soon spreads to create wonderful ground cover. Divide overgrown clumps in spring or autumn.	• Self-heal thrives on fairly poor soils, so don't overfeed or grow on a very rich soil. • Among my favourites are *P. grandiflora* itself (violet), 'Loveliness' (lilac), 'Pink Loveliness', 'White Loveliness' and 'Rotkäppchen' (deep carmine).
Well-drained soil (especially in winter), in plenty of sun.	Best planted in spring – it needs regular watering to establish well, but cold and wet together makes it rot. Divide large clumps in spring.	• Set plants slightly above ground level to stop water puddling around the base. • Once established, sisyrinchiums have a tendency to self-seed, producing variable offspring in such quantity that they may become a nuisance.
Well-fed soil, in a sunny position.	An extremely easy plant to grow, it is best planted in mild spells during spring or autumn. Divide established clumps in autumn or spring.	• Most of the named varieties are smaller and more compact than the species. I particularly like 'Carmine Glow' (warm carmine), 'Caerulea Plena' (double, deep blue flowers), 'Isis' (light blue) and 'Zwanenburg Blue' (pinkish-lilac).

SUMMER MAGIC
The sword-shaped leaves of *Sisyrinchium striatum* are often mistaken for those of iris, but the wands of delicate flowers are quite different.

TALL STORY
With a common name like spider flower, the strange but very striking appearance of *Cleome* in bloom comes as no surprise. Very useful for height in summer bedding.

MASS PRODUCTION
The loose flower spikes of *Diascia barberae* 'Blackthorn Apricot' are so plentiful that they create a wonderful mound of colour.

Flowering climbers

WITHOUT HEIGHT, even an otherwise interesting garden can seem dull. By clothing arches, arbours, trellis, walls and fences with climbing plants, any plot, large or small, becomes more exciting. Careful positioning also allows you to hide ugly features in or beyond the garden.

OTHER FLOWERING CLIMBERS

Clematis (*Clematis*) pp.118–19
Fremontodendron pp.140–1
Jasminum nudiflorum pp.150–1

Perennial pea (*Lathyrus latifolius*) pp.132–3
Sweet peas (*Lathyrus odoratus*) pp.56–7

BOLD AND BRIGHT
Provided host plants are sturdy and won't be swamped, let climbers scramble over them for stunning combinations, such as this *Tropaeolum speciosum* in a dark conifer.

Stamens and ovary have an elaborate and unusual structure

Exotic bowl-shaped flowers

A SPECIAL PASSION
Even from a distance the striking flowers of *Passiflora caerulea* have considerable impact, but a closer look reveals just how extraordinary they are.

PLANT	SIZE	APPEARANCE
TRUMPET VINE *Campis radicans*	H 9m (30ft) S 90cm (3ft)	Clusters of gorgeous, bright orange-red trumpet-shaped flowers, each up to 7.5cm (3in) long, develop during late summer and early autumn. Trumpet vines are hardy except in very cold or exposed gardens.
CUP-AND-SAUCER VINE *Cobaea scandens*	H 3m (10ft) S 1.5m (5ft)	In just a single season, cup-and-saucer vine is smothered in extraordinary, cup-shaped, fragrant flowers from mid-summer until autumn, so this tender perennial is usually grown as a half-hardy annual.
CHILEAN GLORY VINE *Eccremocarpus scaber*	H 3m (10ft) S 90cm (3ft)	This fabulously exotic, half-hardy climber is covered in bunches of almost tubular orange flowers with yellow lips throughout the summer and into autumn. It is fast-growing and uses its tendrils to cling to supports.
MORNING GLORY *Ipomoea*	H 2.5–4m (8–13ft) S 90cm (3ft)	Large numbers of spreading, trumpet-shaped flowers in pink, red, blue, purple or white appear from summer right through until early autumn. Fast-growing: grow from seed each year as a half-hardy annual.
SUMMER JASMINE *Jasminum officinale*	H 8m (27ft) S 3m (10ft)	If you like scent in the garden, you can't be without a jasmine! From mid-summer to early autumn this slow-growing, deciduous climber is covered in starry, trumpet-shaped, exquisitely perfumed white flowers.
HONEYSUCKLE *Lonicera*	H 1.5–4m (5–13ft) S 1.5–2.4m (5–8ft)	There are many good species and varieties of these tough, woody perennial climbers, with their delicate yet elaborate, fragrant flowers. Some flower as early as late spring, others bloom into early autumn.
BLUE PASSION FLOWER *Passiflora caerulea*	H 10m (33ft) S 1.2m (4ft)	Nothing quite prepares you for the strange beauty of passion flowers – white, pink or purple-tinged, with an intricate central display, borne from mid-summer to early autumn. Much hardier than it looks.
CHILEAN POTATO VINE *Solanum crispum*	H 4m (13ft) S 90cm (3ft)	This pretty scrambling plant produces numerous star-shaped, delicately fragrant purple flowers with yellow stamens from mid-summer until early autumn. It is hardy only in mild areas or if protected.
FLAME CREEPER *Tropaeolum speciosum*	H 3m (10ft) S 60cm (2ft)	An attractive hardy herbaceous perennial climber, covered in long-spurred, trumpet-shaped flame-red flowers from mid- to late summer. Flowers are often followed by bright blue berries in autumn.
Tropaeolum tuberosum	H 3m (10ft) S 60cm (2ft)	This fast-growing, half-hardy herbaceous perennial climber produces elongated, bright orange-red flowers, each up to 4cm (1½in) long, from mid-summer until early autumn. The foliage is prettily lobed and grey-green.

SITE	CULTIVATION	HINTS AND TIPS
A sunny, sheltered spot and moist, free-draining soil.	Ideally, plant at the end of summer or in early spring and feed and water regularly. Provide a support, such as a wall, to which the creeper can cling.	• Choose a sunny wall, which will provide adequate protection over winter and allow plenty of flowers to develop. Water regularly. • Trumpet vines are slow-growing; expect a plant to be about 1.8m (6ft) high after five years.
Plant in well-drained soil, in a sunny spot sheltered from wind.	Plant in early summer and provide netting or wires for it to scramble up. Rapid growth makes it a hungry feeder, and plenty of water is important.	• Raise from seed sown in individual pots in a warm greenhouse in late winter or early spring. • The flowers open creamy-green and age to purple. The variety 'Alba' has white flowers turning to cream.
Well-drained soil, in sun.	Best planted in spring and treated as a half-hardy annual. If you provide winter protection for the base of the plant, it may regrow in the spring.	• The Chilean glory vine is a rampant self-seeder, so its tenderness is rarely a problem as many seedlings usually appear in spring and rapidly grow to replace plants killed by frost. • Anglia hybrids come in a range of flower colours.
A sheltered, sunny spot with any reasonable soil.	Sow seed in a heated propagator in early to mid-spring and plant out as soon as all frosts are over. Provide support with wires, trellis or other plants.	• Grown in dappled shade, flowering is reduced, but you still get a pretty show. • Soak seeds in water overnight before sowing to speed up germination and increase success. • I. tricolor 'Heavenly Blue' has the best blue flowers.
A well-drained soil is best, in sun or part shade.	Plant in spring or summer. It twines, so needs a support of thin wires or struts, such as a trellis or other framework. Take semi-ripe cuttings in summer.	• Don't panic about its ultimate size – jasmine takes about five years before it reaches 3.5m (12ft). • For delightfully variegated foliage that gives the whole plant a shimmering, silvery look, choose the variety 'Argenteovariegatum'.
Not fussy; avoid poorly draining or too-dry soil. Needs sun or dappled shade.	Ideally, plant honeysuckles in spring or autumn, if possible with the roots in the shade. Water and feed regularly in spring and early summer.	• Fantastic climbers for a pergola or arbour where you can readily enjoy the fragrance. • Routine pruning is not necessary, but thin out straggly plants and reduce large ones by pruning in spring, or in autumn in warm areas.
Well-drained soil, in full sun.	Best planted in spring against a wall in all-day or afternoon sun in a sheltered position. It will need to be given supports to clamber up.	• Protect in winter in the first few years and during harsh winters. If the stems are killed by frost, the plant almost always reshoots from the base. • After flowering, the plant may produce yellow-orange fruits, edible but seldom worth eating.
Needs a very sheltered spot with plenty of sun and well-drained soil.	Preferably plant in spring; add extra grit to the planting hole to encourage good drainage in all but the best-drained soils. Water frequently during summer.	• You must provide a trellis or system of wires to which the plant can attach itself. • For protection, try a winter "blanket" of dry leaves or straw held in place with chicken wire. • For deep purple-blue flowers choose 'Glasnevin'.
A sunny position with well-drained but moist soil.	Plant in spring. Keep the roots moist during the summer. The roots spread to make new plants; divide in early spring, or sow seed under glass in spring.	• Flame creepers need a framework over which they can scramble. Use them to brighten up existing shrubs or climbers, or along hedges; because the roots run along under the ground, plants pop up in different places each year.
Plant in well-drained yet moist soil, in plenty of sun.	Lift the tubers in early winter and store them in dry compost or bark chippings in a cool but frost-free shed. Separate tubers in early autumn.	• One of the quickest ways of covering bare trellis with flowers, perhaps while slower-growing plants mature. • Slugs like to eat young growth, so if necessary take precautions, particularly early in the season.

EARLY VISITOR
Why not grow morning glory (here, *Ipomoea hederacea*) to create a quick wall of colour whilst longer-lasting woody climbers get established?

SWEET SIMPLICITY
The simple white flowers of *Jasminum officinale* 'Argenteovariegatum' help to lighten a slightly shady spot, especially as they are combined with variegated foliage.

ORIENTAL BEAUTY
The deeply fragrant Japanese honeysuckle (*Lonicera japonica*) is all restrained elegance.

Easy annuals

CHOOSE ANY OF THE plants here and you can "direct sow" them straight into your garden soil without having to bother with seed trays, compost or a propagator. Sow at intervals in spring (with some you can start the previous autumn), and they'll put on a superb show all through the summer.

OTHER ANNUALS TO SOW DIRECT

Baby's breath (*Gypsophila*) pp.150–1
Sunflowers (*Helianthus*) pp.82–3
Morning glory (*Ipomoea*) pp.134–5

Sweet peas (*Lathyrus odoratus*) pp.56–7
Poppies (*Papaver*) pp.110–11
Scabious (*Scabiosa*) pp.150–1

DAY OF THE TRIFFIDS
Who says triffids are ugly or frightening? The beautiful pinky-purple flowers of *Malope trifida* more than make up for its Latin name!

HISTORY LESSON
The dazzlingly bright flowers of pot marigolds are always a welcome sight and have been popular in the garden for centuries – they are featured in the reconstructed early 18th-century Privy Garden at Hampton Court Palace.

PLANT	SIZE	APPEARANCE
POT MARIGOLDS *Calendula officinalis*	H 20cm (8in) S 30cm (12in)	Favourites with children, pot marigolds have orange, cream or yellow daisy- or pompon-like flowers from early to late summer. The foliage is divided and strongly aromatic – said by some to deter cats!
CANDYTUFT *Iberis amara*	H 25cm (10in) S 15cm (6in)	With its slightly fragrant, dome-shaped heads of small, white, lilac or pink flowers, candytuft is a magnet for butterflies and beneficial insects such as hoverflies. This hardy annual blooms throughout summer.
ANNUAL MALLOW *Lavatera trimestris*	H 60–90cm (2–3ft) S 45m (18in)	Choose mallow if you want a plant that instantly looks as if it's been there forever. This sturdy, bushy hardy annual is covered in pink flowers up to 10cm (4in) across from mid-summer to early autumn.
POACHED EGG PLANT *Limnanthes douglasii*	H 15cm (6in) S 15cm (6in)	This plant's common name perfectly describes its flowers, with bright egg-yolk yellow centres surrounded by white petals. Bees love it, and it brings a splash of colour from late spring until the end of summer.
FLAX *Linum grandiflorum*	H 30–45cm (12–18in) S 7.5cm (3in)	Large numbers of small, saucer-shaped pale pink flowers are produced by the flax plant from mid- to late summer. The stems and foliage of this hardy annual are a lovely complementary delicate green.
VIRGINIAN STOCK *Malcolmia maritima*	H 20cm (10in) S 30cm (12in)	These are some of the simplest and quickest hardy annuals to grow, often flowering just one month after spring sowing to form delicate clouds of scented flowers in shades of pink, red, white or purple.
MALOPE *Malope trifida*	H 90cm (3ft) S 30cm (12in)	If you enjoy cutting flowers to take indoors make room for malope in your border. Its large pinky-purple flowers, marked with dark purple veins, are in plentiful supply from mid-summer to mid-autumn.
NIGHT-SCENTED STOCK *Matthiola bicornis*	H 30cm (12in) S 25cm (10in)	Not as showy as other commonly grown stocks, but wait until dusk and you'll be won over by its intense, sweet perfume. This hardy annual produces spikes of lilac flowers from mid- to late summer.
BABY BLUE-EYES *Nemophila menziesii*	H 45cm (18in) S 30cm (12in)	A quaint name for a pretty plant, baby blue-eyes produces a mass of sky-blue flowers with white centres throughout summer until autumn – it's one of the longest-flowering hardy annuals.
MIGNONETTE *Reseda odorata*	H 30–60cm (12–24in) S 15cm (6in)	This has a sensational fragrance, from dense spikes of minute greenish-yellow or pale brown flowers. A hardy annual loved by butterflies, it will grace your border from mid-summer until early autumn.

SITE	CULTIVATION	HINTS AND TIPS
Plant in well-drained soil, in full sun. Ideal for containers.	Sow in early to mid-spring; thin seedlings to 45–60cm (18–24in) apart. Sow at one- or two-week intervals to ensure a longer flowering period.	• Pot marigolds do not flower well if over-watered, or during warm, humid weather. Avoid later sowings if you expect these conditions. • I particularly like 'Radio Extra Selected', with its bright orange blooms, and 'Apricot Pygmy'.
Well-drained soil, in a sunny position.	Best sown direct in early or mid-spring (they dislike being sown in seed trays). Candytuft performs better than most annuals in a dry situation.	• Sow in drifts or clumps between larger plants. • 'Dwarf Fairyland Mixed' produces plants 20–25cm (8–10in) tall, with a mixture of maroon, carmine, lilac and white flowers. • Collect the seedheads to use in dried displays.
Excellent for a dry, sunny site – against a sunny wall, perhaps.	Sow seed in early to mid-spring; thin seedlings to 45cm (18in) apart. Water young plants regularly; established plants are fairly drought-tolerant.	• Keep an eye out for aphids, which often attack tender young growth. • My favourite varieties are 'Silver Cup', with bright pink flowers, the pure white 'Mont Blanc', and the cerise-pink 'Ruby Regis'.
Moisture-retentive soil, in sun.	Sow seed in early spring or the previous autumn and thin out to about 15cm (6in) apart. Keep seedlings and plants well watered. Will self-seed.	• Very easily grown and quick to flower: a great gap-filler in a perennial border. • Good as border edging or on a rockery area. • Plant close to roses – the larvae of the hoverflies they attract will devour aphids.
Choose a sunny spot with well-drained soil.	Best sown early spring or early the previous autumn. Thin seedlings to about 13cm (5in) apart, close enough to grow into each other but not cramped.	• *Linum grandiflorum* 'Album' has pure white flowers (4cm/1⅓in wide), readily producing them in loose clusters. • For something more fiery, *L. rubrum* has beautiful, satiny-red flowers with dark centres.
Any site with well-drained soil, in plenty of sun.	Sown in spring, these stocks will usually flower just a few weeks later. Seed can also be sown in autumn for flowers the next summer.	• Sow batches of seed every two weeks or so to enjoy the flowers and fragrance of Virginian stocks throughout the summer. • Drizzle seed into soil-filled gaps between paving for splashes of cottage garden-style colour.
Any soil will do, but make sure that malopes get plenty of sun.	Sow in mid-spring and thin seedlings to about 30cm (12in) apart. Prompt removal of faded flowers will increase the length of the flowering period.	• I love 'Pink Queen', with shell-pink flowers, and 'White Queen', with pure white flowers. Each grows to a stately 60–90cm (2–3ft). • For a lovely mixture of pink, white, red and purple flowers, try 'Large Flowered Hybrids'.
A sunny or partly shaded spot with well-fertilized, moist soil.	Sow in late spring, in drifts or among other annuals or perennials. Thin seedlings to about 20–25cm (8–10in) apart. Keep well watered at all times.	• Position stocks close to open windows, arbours or other areas where you may sit in the evening. • Add seeds to hanging baskets and other containers. For really showy pink flowers, look out for the variety 'Pink Scentsation'.
Moisture-retentive soil, in sun or part shade.	Sow in early to mid-spring and keep seedlings and plants well watered. I use twiggy sticks to support these plants, as they tend to flop.	• Baby blue-eyes are good in containers as well as in borders, but keep them well watered. • For contrast, 'Total Eclipse' is nearly black with a neat white edge to the petals; 'Pale Face' is white and covered in tiny black freckles.
Well-drained soil, in plenty of sun.	Sow in mid- to late spring; if the weather is still quite cool, cover with a cloche to keep the soil warm. Thin seedlings to 30cm (12in) apart.	• Mignonette grows rapidly, so several planted together produce a really fast gap filler. • If you want a more showy plant, choose 'Fragrant Beauty', which has lime-green flowers with a distinct red tinge.

SOFT TOUCH
The delicate-looking flowers of *Linum grandiflorum* 'Rubrum' belie its hardy nature; it can be sown in autumn for early blooms.

HIGH AND DRY
Grown primarily for its perfume, *Reseda odorata* is perfect for a dry situation close to a patio or terrace.

CHOICE SELECTION
An annual relative of the shrubby lavatera, *Lavatera trimestris* 'Pink Beauty' is a lovely true pink.

Flowers for bees and butterflies

BEES AND BUTTERFLIES are a welcome sight in any garden, and by planting flowers that they find attractive, you can be sure that you will have plenty of these small visitors for as long as the plants are in bloom. The pollinating activity of the bees will also be welcome if you grow produce.

OTHER FLOWERS FOR BEES AND BUTTERFLIES

Perennial asters (*Aster*) pp.78–9
Foxgloves (*Digitalis*) pp.42–3
Eryngiums (*Eryngium*) pp.68–9

Sweet peas (*Lathyrus odoratus*) pp.56–7
Lavender (*Lavandula*) pp.70–1
Ice plants (*Sedum spectabile*) pp.156–7

PRETTY RICH *left*
Butterflies love pinks and mauves – here *Origanum laevigatum* 'Herrenhausen' has attractively tinted foliage that adds to the rich mid-purple of the flowers.

MOONSTRUCK *below*
This *Coreopsis verticillata* 'Moonbeam' looks as if it might blow away in a puff of wind, yet its stems will bear the weight of a bumbling bee.

PLANT	SIZE	APPEARANCE
THRIFTS *Armeria*	H 60–120cm (2–4ft) S 30–45cm (12–18in)	Who wouldn't be drawn to these delightful evergreen hardy perennials? From the end of spring until mid-summer they form mounds of pink or white, near-spherical flowerheads on long, straight stems.
PERENNIAL COREOPSIS *Coreopsis*	H 30–60cm (12–24in) S 45cm (18in)	You can rely on coreopsis to produce a profusion of golden-yellow flowers, either single or double, for much of the summer and into early autumn. Although perennial they will need replacing after a few years.
PERENNIAL GAILLARDIAS *Gaillardia*	H 25–75cm (10–30in) S 45cm (18in)	Startling, brightly coloured daisy-like flowers in red, orange or yellow, often bicoloured, are borne by gaillardias for much of the summer and into early or mid-autumn, depending on the variety.
AVENS *Geum chiloense*	H 25–75cm (10–30in) S 25–50cm (10–20in)	The flowers of avens have such innocent, open faces. Hardy perennials, they bear bright orange, red or yellow, single or double flowers, with prominent, usually golden-yellow stamens, throughout the summer.
ROCK ROSES *Helianthemum*	H 20–45cm (8–18in) S 30–60cm (12–24in)	From late spring through until early summer these hardy, shrubby evergreens are covered in beautiful open flowers with delicate petals in dazzling shades of red, orange, yellow, pink or cream.
LIGULARIAS *Ligularia dentata*	H 1.2–1.8m (4–6ft) S 60cm (2ft)	Like golden beacons in the flower border, these imposing hardy perennials have tall, compact spikes of tiny daisy-like flowers in shades of orange or yellow from the middle to the end of summer.
BERGAMOT *Monarda*	H 60–120cm (2–4ft) S 30–45cm (12–18in)	Bees just can't get enough of these unusual tufted flowers in white or shades of pink, purple, mauve or red. These fairly short-lived hardy perennials or biennials bloom for much of the summer.
CATMINT *Nepeta*	H 30–90cm (12–36in) S 60–75cm (24–30in)	Both cats and bees find most species of catmint irresistible. These superb low-growing hardy perennials produce fragile-looking flower spikes in white or shades of purple or lavender all through summer.
OREGANO *Origanum laevigatum*	H 50–60cm (20–24in) S 45cm (18in)	The purple flowers may be tiny, but they are grouped together into impressive flowerheads from mid-summer until mid-autumn. The foliage of this hardy perennial is blue-green and aromatic.
POTENTILLA *Potentilla*	H 45cm (18in) S 60cm (2ft)	These hardy perennials produce masses of pretty red, orange, yellow or pink flowers, which are either single or semi-double. They bloom throughout the summer, set off by attractive, often silvery, foliage.

SITE	CULTIVATION	HINTS AND TIPS
Well-drained soil and plenty of sun.	Best planted in spring, thrifts pretty well look after themselves. Divide established plants in late summer or take semi-ripe cuttings in summer.	• Use thrifts to form neat, colourful edging to paths, borders and steps. They are also at home in alpine troughs or rock gardens. Many thrifts are maritime plants, so they stand up well to buffeting by the wind.
Prefer a sunny spot with well-drained soil.	Plant in spring. Coreopsis benefit from being fed with a high-potash fertilizer to ensure plenty of flowers. Support taller plants. Deadhead regularly.	• Hardy annual coreopsis are also available. • Young plants are easily raised from seed sown in a heated propagator in early spring. • For softer colour schemes, the single flowers of *C. rosea* are a lovely pale pink.
Anywhere with well-drained soil and plenty of sun.	Ideally, sow the seed direct into spare ground in spring, grow on, and transfer into their flowering sites the following spring. Divide established plants in spring.	• Taller plants may need supports. • Gaillardias need good drainage to overwinter; even then, their lifespan is only about three years. • Annual gaillardias can be raised from seed sown direct in late spring or early summer.
Need soil that retains moisture but is well drained, ideally in full sun.	Planted in spring or autumn, they are easy to look after. Deadhead regularly to prolong flowering. Divide established plants in autumn or early spring.	• Avens will perform surprisingly well in part or dappled shade, but flowering will be less showy and the plants are likely to become leggier. • For damp, shadier spots try *G. rivale* (water avens), which has pink or cream bell-like flowers.
Well-drained soil and plenty of sun.	Plant in spring, and incorporate extra grit if your soil is not extremely free-draining already. Take semi-ripe cuttings in mid- to late summer.	• Clip over shortly after the flowers have faded to keep growth dense and bushy. • Choose a sheltered site to ensure the most prolific flowering, and to prevent flowers and foliage being spoiled by cold winds.
Dappled shade, sheltered from sun and wind, with moist soil.	Plant in autumn or spring. Incorporate bulky organic matter to improve soil moisture retention. Divide established plants in autumn or spring.	• Tall plants will need support. • Ligularias thrive growing close to ponds as well as in moist borders. • Try 'Othello' for its purplish leaves; 'Desdemona' has browny-green leaves with red-brown undersides.
They need fairly moist soil in either sun or part shade.	Best planted in spring or autumn. If your soil has a tendency to dry out, add bulky organic matter, which will hold moisture, before planting.	• After three or four years bergamots start to decline and are best replaced with fresh plants. • For the most startlingly bright red flowers, choose 'Cambridge Scarlet'. • Divide established plants in spring.
A well-drained site with plenty of sun.	These easy plants are best planted in spring. Deadheading improves flowering. Divide mature plants in early spring, or take softwood cuttings at the end of spring.	• 'Six Hills Giant' is covered in delicate lavender-coloured flower spikes throughout the summer. • As their common name suggests, cats are frequently attracted to these plants – especially *N. cataria* – and enjoy lying or rolling on them!
Well-drained soil and full sun.	Ideally, plant in spring. Incorporate grit to improve drainage if necessary. Divide established clumps, or take softwood cuttings in spring.	• For lots of new plants in spring, sow seeds in a heated propagator in autumn. • As *O. laevigatum* is also a useful culinary herb (often used to flavour Italian dishes), you might want to plant some close to the house.
Need a reasonably well-drained soil and plenty of sun.	Best planted in spring or autumn, potentillas soon form impressive clumps. Divide established plants in early spring.	• Cut off flower stems as soon as the flowers have faded; this can prolong flowering into autumn. • For warm shades, I love 'Gibson's Scarlet' (bright scarlet), 'William Rollison' (semi-double, reddish-orange) and 'Melton' (reddish-pink).

BRIGHT AND BEAUTIFUL
Although less than knee-high, the bright flowers of *Gaillardia* × *grandiflora* 'Kobold' more than compensate for its size.

SUMMER SENSATION
The large, lavender-coloured flowers of *Nepeta sibirica* are loosely packed on upright stems to stunning effect on this tallish catmint.

RED ALERT
Insects are attracted to flat, single flowers; with its dark-centred, almost luminously bright blooms, *Potentilla* 'Gibson's Scarlet' would be hard to miss.

Flowers for dry places

WATER SHORTAGES can have a devastating effect on gardens, but if you grow plants that prefer dry conditions you can still have great-looking borders. The plants here will also thrive in soil that is light and sandy, and love full sun – perfect for hot, dry gardens.

OTHER FLOWERS FOR DRY PLACES

Rock roses (*Cistus*) pp.112–13 Lavender (*Lavandula*) pp.70–1
Sunflowers (*Helianthus*) pp.82–3 Osteospermums (*Osteospermum*) pp.86–7
Red-hot pokers (*Kniphofia*) pp.38–9 Thymes (*Thymus*) pp.130–1

SOME LIKE IT HOT, *right*
Introduce the fiery colours of zinnias into a really hot spot. Here, the flowers of *Zinnia haageana* 'Persian Carpet' are like glowing embers.

TOUSLED CHARMER *left*
The scatty, bright pink flower spikes of *Liatris spicata* so remind me of a "bad hair day"! They look marvellous among plants with bronze or purple foliage.

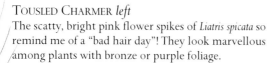

PLANT	SIZE	APPEARANCE
CERATOSTIGMA *Ceratostigma plumbaginoides*	H 45cm (18in) S 60cm (2ft)	Startlingly bright blue flowers burst out all over this shrubby perennial from late summer until the middle of autumn. As a bonus, the deciduous foliage turns bright red in autumn.
SILVER BUSH *Convolvulus cneorum*	H 60cm (2ft) S 60cm (2ft)	This rounded, shrubby plant is usually covered with white funnel-shaped flowers from late spring right through until the end of summer. The downy foliage is an exquisite silvery colour.
Fremontodendron	H 5m (16ft) S 2m (6ft 6in)	The showy, bright yellow flowers of this semi-hardy wall shrub crowd the stems for much of the summer. The leaves are covered in minute bristly hairs and, in mild areas or in mild winters, are semi-evergreen.
GAZANIAS *Gazania*	H 15–30cm (6–12in) S 15–30cm (6–12in)	These tender herbaceous perennials won't survive winter cold, but can easily be grown as annuals. Most bear daisy-like flowers in shades of orange, yellow, red or brown from early summer to mid-autumn.
LEWISIAS *Lewisia cotyledon*	H 30cm (12in) S 30cm (12in)	From late spring to the end of summer these fleshy-leaved hardy perennials produce a good supply of vividly coloured, trumpet-shaped flowers in bright shades of orange, pink, purple, yellow or cream.
GAYFEATHERS *Liatris spicata*	H 60–90cm (2–3ft) S 30cm (12in)	The pink, white or purple flower spikes of gayfeathers look rather like shaggy bottle brushes. In flower throughout the summer, these hardy perennials are also a favourite with butterflies.
DUSTY MILLER *Lychnis coronaria*	H 60cm (2ft) S 45cm (18in)	The silvery, furry foliage makes a lovely backdrop for the bright flowers, in white or shades of pink or reddish-purple, that appear in late summer. This hardy perennial is popular with butterflies.
MEXICAN SUNFLOWER *Tithonia rotundifolia*	H 1.2–3m (4–10ft) S 50–90cm (20–36in)	This less commonly grown sunflower can give traditional *Helianthus* a run for their money, producing delicately scented, bright orange flowers from mid-summer to mid-autumn. It is grown as a half-hardy annual.
YUCCAS *Yucca filamentosa*	H 60–90cm (2–3ft) S 75–90cm (30–36in)	Even when not in flower, you can't miss these dramatic hardy plants with their spiky rosettes of sword-like leaves. The cream-coloured flower spikes rise up to 1.5–1.8m (5–6ft) in mid- to late summer.
ZINNIAS *Zinnia*	H 40–60cm (16–24in) S 30cm (12in)	These dahlia-like flowers have an unabashed exuberance, and come in orange, yellow, reddish-purple, pink or white, flowering from mid-summer to mid-autumn. They are best treated as half-hardy annuals.

SITE	CULTIVATION	HINTS AND TIPS
Choose a warm, dry site with well-drained soil.	Best planted in spring or autumn. If given the protection of a warm wall it will perform to its peak. Divide large plants during the winter.	• May suffer from frost damage, particularly in more exposed sites. Prune only the damaged areas hard back in late spring. • In cold gardens, take semi-ripe cuttings at the end of summer to make new plants, just in case.
A free-draining soil and plenty of sun are essential.	Ideally, plant in spring, adding grit unless the soil is very well drained. Take semi-ripe cuttings with a heel in summer; overwinter in a greenhouse.	• A sheltered site, perhaps close to a wall, is ideal, as it provides protection from winter cold and wet. • This lovely plant is readily killed or reduced to a straggly mess by wet conditions over winter. Improve drainage or grow in a well-drained pot.
Well-drained soil in full sun, preferably with the protection of a warm wall.	Best planted in autumn or spring. No need for routine pruning, but where shoots stick out from the wall, prune back after the main flush of flowers is over.	• If severe weather is forecast, protect with dry bracken or straw held in place with chicken wire. • The hairy stems can cause skin and eye irritation, so wear gloves and goggles when pruning. • Thrives on a chalky or limy soil.
Plenty of sun and good drainage are essential.	Sow seed in a heated propagator in early spring. Harden off, then plant out in late spring or early summer when there is no risk of late frost. Deadhead regularly.	• Gazanias can be kept over frosty winters if you have a greenhouse; lift and pot up in autumn. • Will not flower well in heavily fertilized or recently manured soil. • For a strong display try 'Daybreak Bright Orange'.
Very well-drained acid or neutral soil is essential, ideally in part shade.	Plant in spring, incorporating grit to improve drainage. Increase plant stocks by removing plantlets or dividing the plants in spring.	• Plant slightly shallowly and then surround with a layer of gravel to ensure that excess water does not accumulate around their crowns. • They look great grown in crevices in walls, in rock gardens or on well-drained banks beside steps.
For best results, needs well-drained soil and plenty of sun.	Best planted in spring; add grit to improve drainage on heavier soils. Remove faded flower spikes regularly. Divide established clumps in spring.	• Like many other plants here, they can be grown in part shade, but flowering will be reduced. • For bright white flower spikes choose 'Floristan Weiss', for bright lilac-pink grow 'Kobold', and for purple go for 'Floristan Violett'.
Well-drained soil, in sun or dappled shade.	Best planted in spring; autumn planting should also be successful if the soil is very well drained. Sow seed in a heated propagator in late winter.	• Dusty miller is often rather short-lived, but may be treated as an annual. Seeds started early in a propagator (see left) will flower in their first year. • I particularly like the Alba Group (white) and 'Angel's Blush' (white with a pink flush).
Choose a sunny, sheltered site with well-drained soil.	Sow seed in early spring, prick out into individual pots, harden off, then plant out when any late frosts are over. Taller varieties may need supporting.	• Regular removal of fading flowers prolongs the flowering period. • I like 'Torch', which has vibrant red flowers; for a smaller plant, with deep orange flowers and yellow centres, go for 'Goldfinger'.
Full sun, and soil with good drainage.	Best planted in spring; add grit to improve drainage if necessary. On mature plants, remove suckers with root systems round their bases in spring and plant up.	• Occasionally leaves may be spoiled by fungal leaf spot infections; prune these out or treat with a suitable fungicide. •These drought-tolerant plants are good for pots and will survive a degree of summer neglect.
Well-drained soil and plenty of sun.	Sow in early spring in a heated propagator. After hardening off, plant out when any late frosts are over. Otherwise, sow in late spring direct into the soil.	• Once growing away, zinnias actually prefer not to be watered again. • Regular deadheading prolongs flowering. • Flowering is often disappointing in cool summers – these plants really love a hot, dry spot!

SUN LOVERS
Not for the faint-hearted, these *Gazania* Chansonette Series offer brightly coloured, starry flowers that simply soak up the sun.

SMALL SUCCESSES
Many of the smaller drought-tolerant plants, such as this *Lewisia*, will thrive where little else will grow.

GOOD SHOW
Growing flowering climbers against a very sunny, dry wall can be extremely difficult, but *Fremontodendron* – here 'Pacific Sunset' – provides a colourful and successful solution to the problem.

Flowers for damp places

FACED WITH AN AREA of boggy or wet ground, especially in shade, it's easy to be put off. If there is one secret to gardening, it is to work with rather than against the land, so choose plants that will positively thrive in this environment and you can be sure of a beautiful display.

OTHER FLOWERS FOR DAMP PLACES

Montbretias (*Crocosmia*) pp.156—7
Dicentras (*Dicentra*) pp.98—9
Daylilies (*Hemerocallis*) pp.156—7
Hostas (*Hosta*) pp.158—9
Loosestrife (*Lythrum salicaria*) pp.132—3
Foam flower (*Tiarella cordifolia*) pp.160—1

BIG AND BOLD *right*
There are lots of different species and varieties of filipendula for damp areas, all with interesting foliage topped by unruly flowerheads. Here, *Filipendula purpurea* is used to provide ground cover.

WATER BABIES *below*
In any moist soil astilbes can be guaranteed to produce a mass of foliage and extraordinary flowers. Here, *Astilbe chinensis* var. *taquetii* 'Purpurlanze' blooms in pinky-purple.

PLANT	SIZE	APPEARANCE
ASTILBE *Astilbe*	H 30—60cm (12—24in) S 40—90cm (16—36in)	Similar in shape to ostrich plumes, feather spikes of tiny flowers in white, yellow, purple red or pink appear throughout the summer. This hardy perennial has many good named varieties, all with attractive, divided foliage.
MARSH MARIGOLD *Caltha palustris*	H 40cm (16in) S 50cm (20in)	The golden-yellow buttercup-like flowers of this hardy perennial bring a glorious splash of colour into boggy areas in spring. The large, glossy, kidney-shaped leaves are an added bonus.
SHOOTING STARS *Dodecatheon*	H 45—60cm (18—24in) S 20—30cm (8—12in)	Unusual nodding flowers with swept-back petals and prominent stamens are carried on tall spikes. These hardy herbaceous perennials flower in white, purple, magenta or pink, from early to late spring.
MEADOWSWEET *Filipendula*	H 30—60cm (12—24in) S 30—45cm (12—18in)	These eye-catching perennials flower from mid- to late summer. 'Kahome' is my favourite, for its combination of bright pink, almost frothy-looking flowerheads and attractive, bright green foliage.
YELLOW FLAG *Iris pseudacorus*	H 60—150cm (2—5ft) S 60—90cm (2—3ft)	Bold, bright yellow flowers are produced towards the end of spring, surrounded by fans of sword-shaped leaves. If you can grow yellow flag in shallow water, it should reach even greater heights.
CARDINAL FLOWER *Lobelia cardinalis*	H 60—90cm (2—3ft) S 20—25cm (8—10in)	This perennial lobelia will bowl you over with its showy spikes of bright scarlet blooms and intrigue you with its purple-green foliage and stems. A half-hardy herbaceous plant, it flowers in mid- to late summer.
SCARLET MONKEY FLOWER *Mimulus cardinalis*	H 90cm (3ft) S 60cm (2ft)	The common name suggests something exotic and colourful, and this herbaceous perennial doesn't disappoint with its yellow-throated, dazzling orange-red flowers which bloom throughout the summer.
RANUNCULUS *Ranunculus aconitifolius*	H 60cm (2ft) S 45cm (18in)	The white flowers of this hardy perennial appear in great quantity from late spring through until mid-summer. In the double variety 'Flore Pleno' they are so crowded with petals that they resemble tiny pompons.
GLOBEFLOWERS *Trollius × cultorum*	H 90cm (3ft) S 60cm (2ft)	From late spring to early or mid-summer, showy yellow or orange flowers brighten up any moist or slightly boggy site. The leaves of these herbaceous perennials resemble those of their relative, the buttercup.
ARUM LILY *Zantedeschia aethiopica*	H 75—90cm (30—36in) S 50—60cm (20—24in)	'Crowborough' has to be the star among arum lilies, with its elegant white spathes surrounding a thin yellow flower spike. It flowers from mid-spring until early summer and is hardy except in the harshest winters.

SITE	CULTIVATION	HINTS AND TIPS
Rich, well-fertilized, moist soil is essential. Part shade is best.	Plant in autumn or spring; spacing depends on the variety chosen. Water regularly if the soil is not naturally moist. Divide established plants in the autumn.	• Don't remove the spikes once they are faded; they turn a rich, handsome brown for the autumn and winter. • Occasionally, late frosts spoil the flowers, so consider using fleece to protect them.
Moist or even boggy soil, in a sunny position.	Plant in autumn or spring, watering in well in all but the wettest sites. If possible, plant so that the roots are shaded from the heat of the sun.	• You can divide established clumps in the autumn or as soon as flowering is over. • Marsh marigolds will perform beautifully standing in up to about 12.5cm (5in) of water, so plant them in your pond or pool, too.
A moist but not waterlogged spot in full sun or dappled shade.	Plant in autumn or spring; if the soil is not very moisture-retentive, add plenty of bulky organic matter. A cool, partly shaded spot is best.	• Never allow the soil to dry out. • Slugs and snails may be a problem early in the year, so take precautions if necessary. • Divide established clumps in early spring or as soon as the flowers have faded.
Needs moist or even boggy soil, in sun or part shade.	Best planted in autumn or spring. Keep well watered, especially early on and if the soil shows any sign of drying out. Apply a mulch if growing in sun.	• For more unusual foliage, try *F. ulmaria* 'Aurea', which has golden leaves. It's also much larger, growing to 1.5m (5ft) tall. • Divide plants in mid-autumn or very early spring if you want to increase your stocks.
Thrives in moist soil, or in water up to 45cm (18in) deep, in sun or part shade.	Ideally, plant in autumn or early spring. Provided it has enough water, it is easy to look after. Planting in pond baskets makes lifting and dividing easier.	• Divide every three or four years, as this helps to keep the clumps vigorous and flowering well. • To keep yellow flags at a manageable size for small ponds, always use pond baskets; growing freely in water, they can become much too large.
Requires moist-to-boggy soil in sun or part shade.	Plant in spring. Add plenty of bulky organic matter and water well if the soil tends to dry out in summer. Divide established clumps in spring.	• Ideally, protect the crowns over winter with a deep mulch of chipped bark or bracken held in place with a dome of chicken wire. • Although very showy, the cardinal flower is fairly short-lived, even in ideal growing conditions.
Moist, fertile soil, in sun or part shade. Prefers slightly acid soil.	Best planted in autumn or early spring; add bulky organic matter to the planting hole and water and mulch well, especially during summer, until established.	• Divide established clumps in either autumn or early to mid-spring. • The flowers attract bees and other insects, too. • Check labels carefully – some types of monkey flower are much larger and potentially invasive.
Needs a boggy soil, in sun or dappled shade.	Ideally, plant in autumn or spring; add leafmould or well-rotted manure. Divide established clumps as soon as the flowers have faded.	• Regular deadheading should encourage more flowers to be produced. • During dry spells check that the soil is not drying out at all, and water if necessary. Consider mulching moist soil, too.
A moist site, in sun or part shade.	Best planted in early to mid-autumn. Keep the soil moist at all times and deadhead to ensure the flowering period is as long as possible.	• Divide established clumps in early to mid-autumn. • Although related to buttercups, globe flowers are not invasive. • My favourite varieties are 'Orange Princess' (deep orange) and 'Lemon Queen' (pale yellow).
Moist or boggy soil, or even a shallow pond margin, in sun or part shade.	Easiest to establish if planted in early spring. In moist soils plant about 10cm (4in) deep; if grown in water, plant in a pond basket in up to 15cm (6in) of water.	• Divide established clumps of rhizomes towards the end of summer. • Provide winter protection by deep mulching. • If grown in water, do not let it freeze over – or lift and store plants in baskets.

IN THE SWIM
Unlike most of its relatives, *Iris pseudacorus* will thrive in damp or even wet conditions.

MONKEY BUSINESS
For a splash of screaming scarlet in a damp spot, *Mimulus cardinalis* is a perfect choice. For a less startling effect, there are named varieties in subtler yellow, cream and orange.

FALLING STARS
The flowers of shooting stars (*Dodecatheon*) really do look like tiny heavenly bodies plunging towards the ground.

Flowers for shade

HAVING ONCE gardened under an army of trees, I know how frustrating it can be to work in shady conditions. If you try to grow sun-loving plants they'll never perform as you want them to, but fortunately there are plenty of plants that will bring welcome splashes of flower colour to shade.

OTHER FLOWERS FOR SHADE

BROUGHT TO LIGHT *above*
A shady spot in the garden need not lack colour. Here, *Corydalis flexuosa, Thalictrum, Dicentra* and *Milium effusum* 'Aureum', also known as Bowles' golden grass, light up the whole area.

FAME IS THE SPUR *left*
There are blue, purplish-red and pink forms of *Corydalis flexuosa* from which to make your choice.

PLANT	SIZE	APPEARANCE
ELEPHANT'S EARS *Bergenia*	H 30−45cm (12−18in) S 30−45cm (12−18in)	It's not surprising these hardy perennials ar so widely grown – their evergreen foliage makes good ground cover, they thrive in shade, and they produce masses of spring flowers in white or shades of pink.
BUGBANE *Cimicifuga simplex*	H 1.2−1.5m (4−5ft) S 60cm (2ft)	From late summer until mid-autumn, thes tall, hardy herbaceous perennials produce plentiful supply of elegant, often slightly arching spires, each made up of numerous tiny, white or cream star-shaped flowers.
CORYDALIS *Corydalis solida, C. flexuosa*	H 20−30cm (8−12in) S 20−30cm (8−12in)	Dainty foliage is topped by clusters of equally delicate, spurred flowers from earl spring until early summer. These perennial are naturally carpet-forming, with flowers in shades of blue, pink, purple or red.
LEOPARD'S BANE *Doronicum*	H 40−60cm (16−24in) S 40−45cm (16−18in)	Leopard's bane is amazingly versatile. It wi brighten a shady border in spring or early summer, but you can grow this yellow-flowered, daisy-like hardy herbaceous perennial almost anywhere.
EPIMEDIUMS *Epimedium*	H 20−40cm (8−16in) S 20−30cm (8−12in)	You couldn't ask for more graceful flowers than these low-growing, hardy, herbaceou or evergreen perennials. In spring, exquisi saucer- or cup-shaped flowers bloom in whi or shades of pink, purple, yellow or red.
DOG'S TOOTH VIOLETS *Erythronium*	H 15−30cm (6−12in) S 15−30cm (6−12in)	These nodding, trumpet-shaped flowers, often with petals that curve backwards, bring great elegance to the garden from mid- to late spring. Fully hardy bulbs, they flower in white, lilac, pink or yellow.
MEADOWSWEET *Filipendula*	H 60−180cm (2−6ft) S 45−60cm (18−24in)	Tiny, fluffy flowers in white, pink, red or cream form such a mass of feathery plume that they look like clouds floating above the plants. These hardy herbaceous perennials flower throughout the summe
BUSY LIZZIES *Impatiens walleriana* hybrids	H 20−30cm (8−12in) S 20−30cm (8−12in)	Busy lizzies are best treated as half-hardy annuals and raised or bought fresh every year. They form dense mounds of flowers, pink, red, white, purple or bicoloured, for much of the summer and early autumn.
WOOD LILIES *Trillium*	H 15−60cm (6−24in) S 10−45cm (4−18in)	Distinctive, three-petalled flowers are held singly above a set of three leaves. These choice hardy herbaceous perennials flower between mid-spring and very early summe in white, pink, maroon or a greenish-yellov
WALDSTEINIA *Waldsteinia ternata*	H 15cm (6in) S 45cm (18in)	Diminutive saucer-shaped flowers in brigh yellow carpet the ground in profusion in early summer. Each flower of this charming evergreen perennial has a prominent mass of golden stamens.

SITE	CULTIVATION	HINTS AND TIPS
Elephant's ears are not too fussy about soil, but they prefer semi-shade.	Ideally, plant in autumn or spring. Although suited to semi-shade, stronger foliage colour develops in sun. Divide mature clumps in spring or autumn.	• Many interesting species are available but generally flower less profusely than named hybrids. • For interesting autumn foliage, try 'Bressingham Ruby' (turns from green to maroon with crimson undersides) or *B. purpurascens* (flushes purple).
A partially shaded spot with a moist, ideally lime-free, soil.	Best planted in autumn or spring, preferably in a sheltered spot. In more exposed sites or if growing taller types, supports may be necessary.	• Divide established clumps in spring or autumn. • You can grow bugbanes in full sun, but there is a danger that the leaves may become scorched. • In dry weather, ensure that plants are kept moist at the roots. Mulching will help, too.
Part shade with well-drained soil full of organic matter is ideal.	Preferably plant in autumn or spring. Add plenty of well-rotted organic matter to improve soil texture. Keep well watered during dry weather.	• The best way to get new specimens is to divide established plants in spring or autumn. • Also try *C. lutea*, which has yellow flowers throughout summer, and look out for *C. flexuosa* 'Purple Leaf', with a purple tinge to its foliage.
Not fussy – will grow in most reasonable soils in shade, part shade or sun.	Ideally, plant in early spring or autumn. After a few years the plants lose vigour, so regular division is advisable in late spring or early winter.	• Thrives on chalky soils. • Deadhead regularly for a longer flowering period. • The deeper the shade, the taller the plant and the greater the likelihood that you will need to use twiggy sticks to support it.
A well-drained yet humus-rich soil, in partial shade or full sun.	Best planted in early spring or autumn, incorporating leafmould if necessary. Divide established plants in early spring or autumn.	• While the plants are establishing, keep them well watered and they will soon grow away. • Excellent for ground cover in the dappled shade beneath shrubs. As an added bonus, the foliage changes colour with the seasons.
Moist soil, rich in organic matter, and partial shade are required.	Autumn is the best time to plant. Don't let the tubers dry out before planting. Choose a spot that shades the plants throughout the summer.	• Divide the tuberous clumps towards the end of summer or in autumn. • For leaves covered in attractive, reddish-brown spots, try *E. dens-canis*, with white, purple or pink flowers, and *E.* 'Pagoda', with yellow flowers.
Moist or even boggy soil, as at the edge of a pond, in part shade or sun.	Ideally, plant in autumn or spring. Feed with a high-potash fertilizer to encourage flowering. Divide established clumps in autumn or early spring.	• For smaller gardens, choose 'Kahome' (60cm/2ft) or *F. palmata* 'Nana' (45cm/18in), both of which have rose-pink flowers. • For a dry site in full sun, try *F. vulgaris*, which has white flowers and thrives in such conditions.
Plant in shade or dappled shade in any reasonable, fertile soil.	Plant out as soon as any frosts are over and keep plants well watered. Buy young plants instead of growing from seed, which can be tricky.	• The shadier the conditions, the taller the plants become. In deep shade they become very leggy. • For larger, showy plants consider the New Guinea hybrids, tender perennials which have variegated pink, yellow and green foliage.
Moist, acid or neutral soil rich in organic matter, in part or full shade.	Best planted in autumn; add plenty of organic matter to improve moisture retention. Sow seed in a cold frame or cold greenhouse in autumn.	• Don't be surprised if newly planted wood lilies take a while to settle in – this is not unusual. • Some wood lilies may be damaged by late frosts, so choose a sheltered spot where possible. • *T. sessile* has scented, reddish-brown flowers.
Well-drained soil, in part shade or sun.	Waldsteinias are easy to grow. Best planted in autumn or spring, they spread rapidly provided the soil is kept moist. Try mixed plantings with bulbs.	• Waldsteinia spreads by producing shoots that then root into the ground, so propagation is easy – just detach rooted sections in late summer. • To ensure plants establish well, grow them on in pots until they produce a strong root system.

HINT OF THE ORIENT
The spiky flowers of erythroniums remind me of colourful pagodas as they hang above the often intricately marbled foliage.

LIGHT IN DARKNESS
Bring interest to a shaded corner with the white flower spikes of *Cimicifuga simplex* 'Brunette'.

DRESSED IN YELLOW
The golden-yellow flowers of *Waldsteinia ternata* make perfect ground cover for a shaded site. Even when it is not in bloom, its evergreen foliage is attractive.

Flowers for chalky soil

CHALKY, ALKALINE soil tends to get a bad press, because it's often assumed that few plants really enjoy these conditions. In fact, there are plenty of lovely, cottage garden-style flowers that will actively thrive on chalk, often doing better than they would if your soil were acid or neutral.

OTHER FLOWERS FOR CHALKY SOIL

Anemones (*Anemone*) pp.108−9
Campanulas (*Campanula*) pp.96−7
Fritillaries (*Fritillaria*) pp.100−1

Peonies (*Paeonia*) pp.54−5
Salvias (*Salvia*) pp.74−5
Verbascums (*Verbascum*) pp.40−1

PARTNERS IN PINK
Try growing *Dianthus* 'Becky Robinson' with other pink-flowered plants, such as *Lobularia maritima* Easter Bonnet Series (*facing page, top*).

LA VIE EN ROSE *right*
Another candidate for a pink scheme, this *Sidalcea* 'Elsie Heugh' combines well with *Physostegia* 'Bouquet Rose', border pinks, valerians, campions, alyssums or gladioli.

TALL ORDER *left*
Large gladiolus hybrids such as this 'Georgette' will need canes to support their flower spikes. To avoid staking, choose dwarf varieties or the smaller, delicate species gladioli.

PLANT	SIZE	APPEARANCE
ANTHEMIS *Anthemis tinctoria*	H 60−80cm (24−32in) S 60−80cm (24−32in)	Ferny, slightly grey-green foliage forms a backdrop to pretty daisy-like flowers in white or yellow, depending on the variety. These herbaceous perennials flower throughout the summer.
VALERIAN *Centranthus ruber*	H 60−75cm (24−30in) S 60−75cm (24−30in)	Clusters of tiny, red or pinkish-red flowers form compact flowerheads that open throughout summer and into autumn. The leaves of this hardy herbaceous perennial are somewhat fleshy and greyish-green.
BORDER PINKS *Dianthus*	H 25−40cm (10−16in) S 20−30cm (8−12in)	I can't think of anything prettier than low border pinks, their flowers like tight, frilly rosettes in pink, purple-red or white, bringing colour and scent to the garden throughout early and mid-summer.
GLADIOLI *Gladiolus*	H 90−120cm (3−4ft) S 15−20cm (6−8in)	Brilliantly showy flowers in the form of open trumpets are packed into large flower spikes in summer. These perennials come in a wide range of colours, including red, pink, orange, yellow, purple and white.
ALYSSUM *Lobularia maritima*	H 10cm (4in) S 20cm (8in)	Small white, pink or near-purple flowers are held in rounded groups, forming an almost solid carpet of colour for much of the summer. As this perennial becomes straggly after its first year, grow it as an annual.
OBEDIENT PLANT *Physostegia*	H 120cm (4ft) S 60cm (2ft)	This rather unusual plant has four-cornered stems topped by spikes of tiny tubular flowers in lavender, pink or white. A hardy herbaceous perennial, it flowers from mid-summer into autumn.
SQUILLS *Scilla siberica*	H 15−20cm (6−8in) S 5−7.5cm (2−3in)	Delicate blue or white flowers hang like miniature bells in loose flower spikes in early spring. These hardy perennial bulbs look delightful planted beneath small shrubs, in containers and in borders.
CHECKER MALLOWS *Sidalcea*	H 60−90cm (2−3ft) S 50cm (20in)	Looking like a cross between shrubby mallows (*Lavatera*) and hollyhocks, these hardy herbaceous perennials produce spires of open, funnel-shaped flowers in pink or white from mid- to late summer.
CAMPION *Silene schafta*	H 15cm (6in) S 30cm (12in)	This semi-evergreen perennial produces a constant supply of pretty, pale pink flowers atop spreading tufts of mid-green foliage from the middle of summer through until early or mid-autumn.
GOLDENROD *Solidago*	H 45−120cm (18−48in) S 25−60cm (10−24in)	As their common name suggests, the prominent feature of these hardy herbaceous perennials is their golden-yellow flower spikes, which are produced from summer into autumn.

SITE	CULTIVATION	HINTS AND TIPS
Choose a sunny spot with well-drained soil.	Best planted in spring or autumn. Plants generally do not require any support. Divide established clumps in spring to reinvigorate them.	• Cut back faded flower stems to keep plants looking good and to encourage further flowering. • Best planted in groups of odd numbers in a herbaceous border. • For white flowers, look for *A. tinctoria* 'Alba'.
Well-drained, chalky or limy soil in plenty of sun.	Ideally, plant valerian in spring, or autumn on very well-drained soil. Divide established clumps in spring every third or fourth year.	• Valerian thrives on poor soil, so avoid feeding it or planting it in ground rich in nutrients. If overfed, the plants tend to become leggy and are best replaced. • A great plant for attracting butterflies.
Any reasonably well-drained, fertile soil, in full sun or part shade.	Planting in early or mid-autumn is best. Unlike carnations, pinks should not need support. Take cuttings from non-flowering side-shoots in early to mid-summer.	• Feed generously to keep plants in good condition and flowering well. Replace once they have become straggly, after a few years. • Pinch out the shoot tips of young plants in spring to stimulate bushy growth.
A sunny site with well-drained soil.	Their corms are best planted in spring, 15cm (6in) deep and 15–20cm (6–8in) apart. Manure before planting, and add grit if the soil is not very free-draining.	• Before frosty winters, lift the slightly tender corms in autumn and dry off in a frost-free shed. Clear off debris and store until the following spring. • Cormlets that are removed and grown on will take up to three years to reach flowering size.
Well-drained soil and plenty of sun.	Sow seeds in early spring in pots or trays in a cold greenhouse or cold frame. Alternatively, buy plants as "bedding strips". Plant out towards the end of spring.	• Remove faded blooms to prolong flowering. • Alyssums self-seed readily; named varieties will not come true, but still produce a good show. • For different, striking colours, try 'Oriental Night', 'Apricot Shades' or 'Wonderland Red'.
Plant in a moist soil rich in organic matter, in sun or dappled shade.	Best planted in autumn or spring. Add plenty of compost or leafmould if your soil is light. Keep watered in dry spells and mulch around the base too.	• This lovely, rapidly growing plant may spread too quickly, so be prepared to divide it every year or two, in spring or autumn. • For bright pink flowers choose 'Vivid'; 'Summer Snow' and 'Crown of Snow' have white flowers.
Moisture-retaining yet free-draining soil in dappled shade.	Plant the bulbs towards the end of summer or in early autumn, at a depth and spacing of 5–7.5cm (2–3in). Add leafmould to encourage moisture retention.	• Squills look good if allowed to naturalize; plant at uneven spacings in a drift-like shape. • To increase your stock or replace plants, divide congested clumps every four years or so. • For bright white flowers choose 'Alba'.
Choose a sunny or part-shaded site in any fairly fertile and moist soil.	Checker mallows are very easy to grow. Ideally, plant in autumn or spring. In dry weather water well and apply a mulch. Divide in spring or autumn.	• For really silky-looking mid-pink flowers choose 'Rose Queen'. *S. candida* has white flowers. • Species can be raised from seed sown in a cold frame or cold greenhouse in early spring. • Checker mallows make good cut flowers.
Plant in well-drained, well-fed soil, in full sun.	Best planted in spring or autumn, campions require little attention. Sow seeds early in spring, or divide established plants in autumn.	• I especially like the variety 'Shell Pink', in a particularly delicate shade. • The flowers attract both butterflies and bees and are especially well suited to plantings with an informal or even wild feel to them.
A sunny or part-shaded spot with well-drained yet moist soil.	Ideally, plant in spring or autumn. They are easy to look after and should not need staking. Divide established clumps every three or four years.	• During dry weather ensure that the soil does not dry out completely. • For a small, compact plant choose 'Golden Thumb' (also known as 'Queenie'), which flowers in late summer.

QUICK AND EASY
Easily raised from seed, alyssums – here *Lobularia maritima* Easter Bonnet Series – grow rapidly to create a carpet of colour. They are also an excellent way of filling gaps between paving or as edging for paths.

HIGH JINKS
Physostegias are excellent plants for the middle or back of a border. You can have them in white or go for a variety such as this 'Bouquet Rose', which has pretty lilac-pink spikes.

Flowers for containers

BY GROWING FLOWERS IN containers, you can plant what you like regardless of the soil in your garden. Tubs and pots also allow you to really get the best from plants in small spaces, while those past their best can be moved so that flowers in season can take centre stage.

OTHER FLOWERS FOR CONTAINERS

Crocuses (*Crocus*) pp.154−5	Dwarf daffodils (*Narcissus*) pp.104−5
Gazanias (*Gazania*) pp.140−1	Nasturtiums (*Tropaeolum majus*) pp.160−1
Busy Lizzies (*Impatiens*) pp.144−5	Pansies and violets (*Viola*) pp.116−17

HIGH FLIERS
With their tendency to grow up then sprawl over, *Brachyscome iberidifolia* varieties − here 'White Splendour' − are ideal for growing in containers.

Pelargoniums bring height to the planting

ROSE-TINTED VIEW *below*
I find most petunias grown on their own too bright for my taste, but combined with more subtle pink flowers these look perfect.

Deadhead petunias often

Terracotta pot coordinates with flower colours

PLANT	SIZE	APPEARANCE
TUBEROUS BEGONIAS *Begonia*	H 30−60cm (12−24in) S 30cm (12in)	The flowers of begonias range from small and delicate to big beauties resembling camellias and may be white, pink, red, yellow, orange or cream. They are borne throughout summer and into early autumn.
BIDENS *Bidens ferulifolia*	H 45−60cm (18−24in) S 45cm (18in)	The combination of starry, daisy-like, bright yellow flowers and ferny foliage makes bidens a superb container plant for the summer. Although perennials, they are best grown as half-hardy annuals.
SWAN RIVER DAISIES *Brachyscome iberidifolia*	H 15−30cm (6−12in) S 15−30cm (6−12in)	One word sums up these delightful daisies − giddy! The flowers of these bushy, half-hardy annuals come in white, blue or purple, all with a bright yellow centre, and appear throughout the summer.
FUCHSIAS *Fuchsia*	Extremely variable, so check label for details.	Pendulous flowers resembling bells or elaborate ballerina skirts in white, red, purple, pink or lilac cover the plants throughout summer and into autumn. These perennials range from tender to hardy.
HEBES (SMALL) *Hebe*	H 30−90cm (12−36in) S 30−75cm (12−30in)	Provided you choose small, hardy species or varieties, these pretty evergreen plants are great in containers. Flower spikes in white or shades of pink, red, purple or blue develop from mid-summer into autumn.
LOBELIA *Lobelia erinus*	H 15cm (6in) S 15cm (6in)	Countless tiny jewel-like flowers, in pale pastels, white or bright shades of blue, red, pink or lilac, cover the stems of this hardy annual in a constant stream of colour from the end of spring until the first frosts.
PELARGONIUMS, POT GERANIUMS *Pelargonium*	H 30−60cm (12−24in) S 20−45cm (8−18in)	The many types of pelargonium are all good in containers. All flower profusely, usually right through summer, in white, pink, red or purple; some have beautifully coloured, shaped or scented leaves too.
PETUNIAS *Petunia*	H 20−30cm (8−12in) S 30−50cm (12−20in)	These uncomplicated, showy plants offer single or double, wide-open trumpet-shaped flowers in white, yellow, pink, red, violet, cream − even green − from early summer until the first frosts.
SUN PLANT *Portulaca grandiflora*	H 15−20cm (6−8in) S 20cm (8in)	As if made from the brightest-coloured silks, these open, rose-like flowers dazzle in shocking pink, red, yellow, orange or white. This half-hardy annual blooms from summer until mid-autumn.
VERBENA *Verbena*	H 20−25cm (8−10in) S 30cm (12in)	Rounded flowerheads in white or shades of pink, purple, cream or red are produced from mid-summer until the first frosts. Best treated as half-hardy annuals. Both upright and trailing forms are available.

SITE	CULTIVATION	HINTS AND TIPS
Reasonably well-drained but moist compost in dappled shade.	Buy as growing plants, or start tubers into growth in pots of fresh compost in early spring. Plant out after any late frosts. Keep compost moist but not wet.	• Feed with high-potash fertilizer. • Begonias are not sun-lovers, so use them in pots where they will look their best – in shade. • Once plants have died back in autumn overwinter tubers in dry compost in a frost-free shed.
Any reasonable soil or compost, in sun or part shade.	Buy as plants, or raise your own by sowing seed in a heated propagator in early spring. Harden off plants and plant out after any danger of late frosts.	• Pinch out the shoot tips of small, home-raised plants when they are 5–7.5cm (2–3in) tall to increase branching and bushiness. • Try 'Golden Goddess', which seems to thrive in all the extremes of summer weather.
Well-drained compost in a very sunny, preferably sheltered spot.	Buy as plants in spring, or sow seed in early spring. Grow plants on and harden off before planting out in late spring. Deadhead regularly to prolong flowering.	• Species and taller varieties may flop over – use twiggy prunings as unobtrusive supports. • Create a drift of hazy, daisy colour using a single variety. J look out for 'Splendour White' or 'Splendour Purple'.
Well-drained compost, in sun or part shade.	Ideally, plant out after any danger of late frosts. Keep well watered and fed, and deadhead regularly. Softwood cuttings taken in late spring root readily.	• Pinching out the tips of the shoots early in the season increases bushiness. • Always check whether plants are hardy or not. Mulch hardy plants in winter; lift tender ones and overwinter in a cool but frost-free greenhouse.
Plenty of sun and well-drained compost.	Hebes are best planted in autumn or spring. They dislike both too much and too little water; good drainage and regular watering are essential.	• Take semi-ripe heeled cuttings towards the end of summer. • Add spring- or autumn-flowering plants at the base of the hebe for a long season of colour. • Cut straggly stems back hard each spring.
Well-drained compost, kept moist, in full sun or part shade.	Buy as plants, or sow seed very early in spring in a heated propagator. Prick out, grow on and harden off before planting out once danger of frosts is over.	• Keep lobelia well watered and fed. • Seedlings are prone to damping-off disease, so water seed trays and young plants with a copper-based fungicide at regular intervals. • Discard plants once they start to look tatty.
Well-drained compost, in a sunny position.	Buy as plants, or raise from seed sown in late winter or from softwood cuttings taken in spring or summer. Harden off before planting out after any late frosts.	• Pelargoniums need plenty of feeding. • Deadhead regularly to encourage more blooms and reduce the risk of grey mould infection. • Choose "basket" or "trailing" forms for hanging baskets, windowboxes or the edges of large pots.
Thrive in well-drained compost, in plenty of sun.	Buy as plants or sow seed in early spring in a heated propagator on the surface of the compost. Prick out, harden off and plant out after any late frosts.	• Feed with a high-potash fertilizer. • The small, pretty flowers of the Carillon Series give a more delicate effect. • Trailing forms can be taller (up to 40cm/16in) and spread out up to 90cm (3ft).
Free-draining compost, in plenty of sun.	Readily available as plants, or sow seed in a heated propagator in early spring, prick out and harden off before planting out after any late frosts.	• Beware of overfeeding. Given too rich a lifestyle, these annuals flower less profusely. • Also great for summer ground cover. • If you fancy a double-flowered form, look for the F2 hybrid 'Calypso'.
Plenty of sun, and will thrive in most soils or composts.	Buy as plants, or sow seed in a heated propagator in early spring. Take softwood cuttings in early summer, if seed is unavailable, and overwinter in a greenhouse.	• After sowing, keep seed in the dark in a heated propagator to increase success of germination. • To prevent powdery mildew, spray with a suitable fungicide. • 'Silver Anne' (pale pink) is a good trailing form.

Ivy-leaved pelargonium

Purple-pink verbena

Trailing lobelia

FULL OF PROMISE
Hanging baskets should be crammed with lots of plants and kept well fed and watered.

ENDURING APPEAL
An evergreen, hardy hebe – here *Hebe* 'Bowles Variety' – provides year-round interest.

RUNNING WILD *below*
Trailing stems can be used to create a pretty effect in containers.

Pale lilac lobelia

Trailing helichrysum

Pot feet ensure good drainage

Flowers for cutting

IF YOU HAVE THE SPACE, it's lovely to be able to grow flowers specifically for cutting to display indoors. Although most garden flowers can be picked, some are particularly well-suited to life in both the border and the vase. By growing your own, you can guarantee your favourites for the home.

OTHER FLOWERS FOR CUTTING

KINGPINS *above*
With the bold, bright flowers of *Arctotis fastuosa* 'Monarch of the Veldt' – each bloom up to 5cm (2in) across – you can bring warmth to any room.

BATS IN THE BELFRY *left*
It is easy to see why *Moluccella laevis* is also known as shell flower. With their somewhat eerie appearance, the flowers also remind me of green bats' ears.

PLANT	SIZE	APPEARANCE
YARROW *Achillea*	H 90cm (3ft) S 60cm (2ft)	Large, round, flattened flowerheads (each up to 15cm/6in across), made up of numerous tiny, bright yellow flowers are produced from mid-summer to early autumn by this hardy perennial.
PERUVIAN LILIES *Alstroemeria*	H 30−100cm (12−40in) S 30−90cm (12−36in)	These exotic, orchid-like flowers are reasonably hardy and very easy to grow. They bloom from mid-summer into late autumn in white, cream, shades of red, orange, yellow or lavender.
AFRICAN DAISIES *Arctotis × hybrida*	H 30−45cm (12−18in) S 30cm (12in)	These startlingly beautiful, daisy-like flowers come in white, red, orange, cream, pink or reddish-browns, and bloom for much of the summer. Although perennials, they are grown as half-hardy annuals in cold climates.
CROWN IMPERIALS *Fritillaria imperialis*	H 1.5m (5ft) S 30cm (12in)	Unusual and striking cut flowers, crown imperials have tall flower spikes each bearing a ring of hanging, tulip-shaped flowers in red, orange or yellow, topped with a tuft of leafy bracts, in early summer.
BABY'S BREATH *Gypsophila paniculata*	H 60−120cm (2−4ft) S 25−100cm (10−40in)	No flower arranger would want to be without baby's breath, with its large, airy, delicate sprays of tiny flowers in white or pale pink. This hardy herbaceous perennial flowers from mid-summer to mid-autumn.
BEARDED IRISES *Iris pallida*	H 60−90cm (2−3ft) S 25−30cm (10−12in)	This species of iris has varieties in almost any colour you could wish for. They all have branched flower stems, bearing at least six flowers, usually with a pleasant perfume, from early to mid-summer.
WINTER JASMINE *Jasminum nudiflorum*	H 4−4.5m (13−15ft) S 1.8−2.1m (6−7ft)	A welcome sight in the depths of winter; pale yellow flowers break out over dark green stems at intervals from the end of autumn until early spring. This hardy plant is best trained as a scrambler against a wall.
BELLS OF IRELAND *Moluccella laevis*	H 60−90cm (2−3ft) S 30cm (12in)	Although its tall stems appear to bear bright green trumpet flowers, these are in fact green collars that encase the tiny, white, fragrant flowers. This half-hardy annual flowers from mid-summer to early autumn.
CHINESE LANTERNS *Physalis alkekengi*	H 60−90cm (2−3ft) S 60−90cm (2−3ft)	Like honesty, physalis is grown as much for its seedcases as for its flowers – bright orange-red, lantern-shaped papery bladders that develop around an inner orange berry. A fast-growing hardy herbaceous perennial.
SCABIOUS *Scabiosa caucasica*	H 45−60cm (18−24in) S 45−60cm (18−24in)	Sometimes known as pincushion flower, this hardy annual blooms in lavender, off-white or, best of all, a really true, pale Wedgwood blue throughout most of the summer.

SITE	CULTIVATION	HINTS AND TIPS
Well-drained soil with plenty of sun.	Plant purchased plants in early spring, or sow seed in a heated propagator in late winter or very early spring. Divide established plants in early spring.	• In exposed conditions, some support for the stems may be necessary. • My absolute favourite for cutting has to be *A. filipendulina* 'Cloth of Gold'. • Yarrows make good dried flowers.
A well-drained soil, in a sheltered, sunny spot.	Before planting, dig in garden compost. Plant once any late frosts are over; the top of each tuberous root should be about 2.5cm (1in) below the surface.	• Divide established clumps in spring. • In autumn, mulch the crowns with a deep layer of chipped bark to provide winter protection. • For best results as a cut flower, pick as soon as the first flowers on the stem open.
Free-draining soil and plenty of sun.	Buy as plants or sow seed in a cold frame in spring. Plant out after any late frosts, watering in well. Once established they enjoy an occasional high-potash feed.	• In dull weather and as evening approaches these flowers often close, but they'll open as soon as the sun is out again. • Seeds are available in single or mixed colours, and they all make great cut flowers.
Fairly heavy soil, in sun or part shade.	Plant in autumn, incorporating lots of bulky garden compost to improve fertility and soil texture. Keep them well-fed and well-watered.	• Crown imperials are difficult to propagate at home, so it is best to buy in new bulbs. • They dislike being disturbed and may fail to flower if not allowed to become well-established. • The flowers smell odd, unpleasant to some.
Needs a well-drained, ideally alkaline or neutral soil and plenty of sun.	Best planted in early spring. Tall varieties will need support; twiggy sticks are unobtrusive. Take softwood cuttings in early summer.	• Removing the flowering stems for use as cut flowers will actually stimulate the plant to produce more. • For a compact plant, try 'Festival White'. 'Bristol Fairy' has double, white flowers.
Well-drained soil (slightly chalky is ideal) with plenty of sun.	Plant the rhizomes between mid-summer and early autumn, setting them in shallowly so that each is half-exposed above the soil surface and facing the sun.	• Clumps can be divided every three or four years; discard the old, central rhizomes and replant newer sections. • Water regularly for the first three or four weeks after planting.
Well-drained soil close to a wall or other vertical surface of any aspect.	Best planted in autumn or spring. Winter jasmine makes an excellent covering for a wall, but it will need a support up which to scramble.	• Semi-ripe cuttings taken in mid- to late summer usually root very easily. • To force early flowering, bring stems into a cool room just as the flower buds have started to fatten and then at intervals throughout the winter.
Choose a sunny spot with well-drained, fertile soil.	Sow seed in a heated propagator in early spring, harden off and plant out after any late frosts. In mild areas, try direct sowing in the flowering site in mid-spring.	• Bells of Ireland not only makes a great cut flower, it also adds interest to any border and can be used in dried arrangements, too. • For drying, cut stems before they start to fade and hang upside down in a well-ventilated shed.
Thrives on any reasonable garden soil, in full sun or part shade.	Best planted in autumn or spring. Divide established plants in winter or early spring. If the stems flop, don't bother staking, as it suits them to look informal.	• Given the right conditions, Chinese lanterns can be invasive, so control if necessary by using a sharp spade to cut around the roots every autumn. • They can also be dried, held upright to ensure that the lanterns dry pointing downwards.
Well-drained soil, in plenty of sun.	Sow seed during spring direct into their flowering positions and thin out to 45–60 (18–24in) apart. Deadhead regularly if necessary.	• Bees and butterflies are attracted to these flowers. • For really intense blue flowers try 'Fama'; it has long flower stems, which makes it particularly good for tall arrangements.

RURAL CHARMS
Introduce a relaxed, country air into the home with a bunch of delightfully informal scabious in a simple jug.

NET GAIN *right*
Even when dried physalis seedcases start to disintegrate, they leave a fascinating net-like "lantern".

CROWNED HEADS
I love crown imperials for bold arrangements, but not in small rooms – the scent is a bit overpowering! Try them in the hall or on the landing.

Dried flowers and seedheads

FLOWERS THAT DRY WELL give pleasure all year round, and attractive seedheads look great in arrangements too. Grow plenty of these so you can leave some on the plant over winter; they'll look dramatic covered in a hoar frost, and birds often appreciate the seeds too.

OTHER FLOWERS FOR DRIED ARRANGEMENTS

Hollyhocks (*Alcea rosea*) pp.44–5
Alliums (*Allium*) pp.50–1
Dictamnus albus pp.130–1

Lavender (*Lavandula*) pp.70–1
Nigellas (*Nigella*) pp.72–3
Physalis alkekengi pp.150–1

Seeds are concealed in silvery cases

LUNAR LEGACY *left and below*
This *Lunaria annua variegata* provides interest for many months on end, with its smartly variegated foliage and pretty pink flowers, followed by silvery seedheads in autumn.

HIGH AND DRY *right*
In summer *Echinops ritro* 'Veitch's Blue' bears globes of tiny purple-lilac flowers, fragments of which remain on faded flowers left on the plant.

PLANT	SIZE	APPEARANCE
BEAR'S BREECHES *Acanthus mollis*	H 1.2m (4ft) S 90cm (3ft)	This hardy perennial has large, architectural divided leaves that die back in autumn and reappear again in spring. The stately flower spikes in pink and white that appear in early summer are excellent for drying.
WINGED EVERLASTING *Ammobium alatum*	H 45–60cm (18–24in) S 45cm (18in)	This half-hardy annual produces masses of small, silvery-white everlasting-type flowers, each of which has a large, bright yellow centre. The flowers are produced on winged stems from early summer to mid-autumn.
PEARL EVERLASTING *Anaphalis margaritacea*	H 60–75cm (24–30in) S 60–75cm (24–30in)	From mid-summer into autumn this fast-growing perennial is studded with clusters of small, papery, white flowers that dry well. The foliage is downy-felted and so appears silvery-grey.
GLOBE THISTLES *Echinops*	H 1.2–1.8m (4–6ft) S 30–90m (12–36in)	Spiky, spherical flowerheads in metallic blue to purple are produced on these fast-growing hardy herbaceous perennials from mid-summer until early autumn. They look very eye-catching in dried displays.
STINKING IRIS *Iris foetidissima*	H 50cm (20in) S 30cm (12in)	Although its greyish-pink early-summer flowers are attractive, the stinking iris reserves a bolder display for autumn, with stunning seedpods that split open to reveal bright orange-red or yellow seeds.
STRAWFLOWERS *Helichrysum bracteatum*	H 40–150cm (16–60in) S 30–40cm (12–16in)	Best grown as annuals, strawflowers produce an array of yellow, gold, pink-orange or reddish-brown flowers from mid-summer to mid-autumn. The flower petals are so papery that they dry particularly well.
STATICE *Limonium sinuatum*	H 30–60cm (12–24in) S 30cm (12in)	Statice grows wild on Mediterranean coasts withstanding hot, salty winds – perfect drying conditions. From mid-summer to early autumn, the elongated flower clusters appear in purple, yellow, white, red or blue.
HONESTY *Lunaria annua*	H 90cm (3ft) S 60cm (2ft)	While the white or purple flowers produced by honesty in early summer are pretty, it's the green and, later, silvery-cream disc-like seed cases of this biennial that really catch the eye.
FEVERFEW *Matricaria*	H 15–60cm (6–24in) S 15–45cm (6–18in)	These half-hardy annuals flower throughout the summer, producing daisy-like single or fluffy double flowers in white or yellow. The bushy foliage is a lovely fresh green, with a smell you either love or hate.
JERUSALEM SAGE *Phlomis fruticosa*	H 90cm (3ft) S 90cm (3ft)	With its clusters of hooded flowers, this reminds me of an oversized deadnettle, but with silvery leaves. Bright yellow flowers are formed through the summer on this shrubby, generally hardy evergreen.

SITE	CULTIVATION	HINTS AND TIPS
Well-drained soil, ideally in full sun, or if not in light shade.	Plant in spring, incorporating grit if the soil has a tendency to become wet in winter. The easiest method of propagation is by division in spring.	• In cold areas, mulch the crown with chipped bark to provide winter protection. • Very prone to powdery mildew disease; if attacks occur early in the season, consider spraying with a suitable fungicide.
Requires well-drained soil and plenty of sun.	Sow seed in a heated propagator from late winter to early spring. Harden off, then plant out after any danger of frost. They need little watering once established.	• Cut just as most of the flowers on the stem are starting to open. • Like other everlasting-type flowers, it is best to tie them loosely into bunches and dry by hanging upside down in a well-ventilated shed.
Well-drained yet moisture-retentive soil, in plenty of sun.	Plant out in autumn or early spring (spring is better if there is any tendency for the soil to be wet over winter). Water well during dry weather.	• Established plants can be divided in spring or autumn. • For smaller spaces, choose the more compact variety 'Neuschnee', which grows to only 45cm (18in) tall, with a similar spread.
Choose a sunny spot with well-drained soil.	Plant in autumn or spring; add grit if the soil is not well-drained. Divide established clumps in spring or autumn, or take root cuttings at the end of autumn.	• Globe thistles attract bees, butterflies and birds. • They perform well in very dry conditions and on poor soils or chalk. • Best picked for drying just before the tiny purple flowers appear.
Needs a reasonably moist soil, in part shade.	Plant towards the end of summer or in early autumn. Divide established clumps in autumn, or collect and sow seeds direct into the flowering site.	• Cut the stems bearing the seedheads just as the pods start to split. Dry them standing up, or else the seeds will all fall out. • The foliage has an unpleasant smell when cut or crushed.
Free-draining soil and plenty of sun.	Plant out in spring. Seed can be sown direct into the flowering position in early to mid-spring, or sown in a heated propagator in early spring.	• Tall varieties may need some support if grown in an exposed position. • Cut for drying just before the flowers are fully open and hang in bunches in a well-ventilated shed or garage.
Well-drained, alkaline or neutral soil, in full sun.	Plant out in spring after any late frosts. Single- or mixed-colour plants may be raised from seed sown in a heated propagator in early spring.	• Dry in bunches hung in a well-ventilated shed or garage. • For smaller gardens, choose 'Dwarf Biedermeier Strain', which grows to only 25–30cm (10–12in). • 'Pastel Shades' offers more subtle colours.
Likes a well-drained soil, in dappled shade.	Best planted in autumn or spring, and easy to grow. Sow seeds direct where they are to flower in spring or early summer for flowers the following year.	• No need to stake. • Cut the flower stems in late summer before seeds have ripened fully, to prevent them from being spoiled by autumn rain or winds. • 'Alba Variegata' has attractive variegated foliage.
Well-drained soil, in full sun or part shade.	Sow seed in spring in a heated propagator. Harden off, then plant out after any danger of frost. Plants also self-seed readily once established.	• Two of my favourites are 'Butterball', which has dense yellow flowers, and 'Bridal Robe', which has double, bright white flowers. • Cut just as the flowers start to open fully and dry in bunches in a well-ventilated shed.
Choose a site in full sun with well-drained soil.	Plant in spring; add plenty of grit in all but the most well-drained soils. No need to prune regularly. Take semi-ripe cuttings in late summer or autumn.	• Winter wet soon kills Jerusalem sage, so if necessary take cuttings and overwinter them in well-drained compost in a cold frame. • Leave some flower stems on plants in the border to be decorated by frost.

Spikelets bear tiny, papery flowers

BRIGHT SPARKS
The bright flower colours of *Limonium sinuatum* Fortress Series *(above)* and 'Forever Gold' *(above right)* are retained well on drying.

Cases split to reveal the seeds

Seedhead of Iris foetidissima

GREAT BALLS OF FIRE *above*
The flowers of *Iris foetidissima* – here *I. foetidissima* var. *citrina* – are beautiful, but the plant's greatest attraction is the bright scarlet or yellow seeds that burst from the large seedheads in autumn.

FOREVER YOUNG *right*
All strawflowers provide long-lasting colour once dried, and will start to fade noticeably only after a couple of years. These are from the King Size series.

Winter and early spring flowers

ALTHOUGH I QUITE enjoy cold winters, I find myself waiting with bated breath for the first sight of snowdrops that tell me spring is on its way. Even in the depths of winter, there's no need for your garden to close down completely – even one or two plants in flower make all the difference.

OTHER FLOWERS FOR WINTER AND EARLY SPRING

Anemones (*Anemone blanda*) pp.108–9
Hellebores (*Helleborus*) pp.114–15
Stinking iris (*Iris foetidissima*) pp.152–3

Some daffodils (*Narcissus*) pp.104–5
Jasminum nudiflorum pp.150–1
Violets and pansies (*Violas*) pp.116–17

FLOWER POWER
The flowers of *Cyclamen coum* and *Galanthus nivalis* may be tiny, but they have a huge impact in the winter garden, when little else is in bloom.

STARSTRUCK *below*
The bright flower colours of crocuses – here, 'Advance' – never cease to amaze me; they seem more in keeping with summer than with winter and early spring. On sunny days, the flowers open like tiny stars.

PLANT	SIZE	APPEARANCE
COMMON DAISIES *Bellis perennis*	H 15–20cm (6–8in) S 20cm (8in)	These jaunty daisies pop up in early spring, their pink, red or white flowers looking like so many miniature drumsticks. You can enjoy these hardy biennials until early summer.
WALLFLOWERS *Cheiranthus cheiri*	H 20–45cm (8–18in) S 15–20cm (6–8in)	For colour and fragrance wallflowers take some beating; biennials with dense spikes of delicately scented flowers in warm shades of red, yellow, orange, purple or bronze from early spring until early summer.
CROCUSES *Crocus*	H 7–10cm (2¾–4in) S 5–7.5cm (2–3in)	The brightly coloured, cup-shaped flowers of these small, hardy corms are a welcome sight in late winter and spring. Crocuses can be single colours such as white, cream or purple, or a combination of two colours
CYCLAMEN *Cyclamen coum*	H 5–7.5cm (2–3in) S 15cm (6in)	Charm epitomized! From mid-winter to early spring these hardy plants produce small, winged flowers in shades of pink, from very pale to screaming magenta. The leaves may be plain green or silver-patterned
WINTER ACONITE *Eranthis hyemalis*	H 15cm (6in) S 15cm (6in)	Golden yellow buttercup-like flowers, each with a bright green "ruff", develop from this hardy tuber. The flowers look breathtakingly beautiful beneath shrubs or trees from late winter into early spring.
WINTER HEATHERS *Erica carnea*	H 15–30cm (6–12in) S 25–60cm (10–24in)	These make brilliant, easy-care ground cover. Compact but numerous flower spikes in white or shades of pink or purple are produced over a mound of evergreen foliage throughout winter and into early spring.
SNOWDROPS *Galanthus nivalis*	H 10–20cm (4–8in) S 5–10cm (2–4in)	Just seeing these little white bells appear from winter into early spring reminds me that winter cold has its compensations. The flowers of this hardy bulb have pretty green markings on their inner petals.
EARLY IRIS *Iris reticulata*	H 15–20cm (6–8in) S 7.5–10cm (3–4in)	Despite its diminutive stature, this hardy iris is difficult to miss! The brilliant purple-blue flowers are streaked with bright yellow and bring a truly dazzling display to the garden in late winter and into early spring.
SPRING SNOWFLAKE *Leucojum vernuum*	H 20–25cm (8–10in) S 15–20cm (6–8in)	An elegant relative of the snowdrop, spring snowflake has nodding, bell-shaped white flowers, with a distinct green spot on the point of each petal. This hardy bulb flowers from late winter to early spring.
PASQUE FLOWERS *Pulsatilla vulgaris*	H 20cm (8in) S 15cm (6in)	One of the most distinctive features of pasque flowers is the silky down that covers their stems and flowers. Delicate bell-shaped flowers appear from early spring, in white, pinkish-red or purple, with golden stamens.

SITE	CULTIVATION	HINTS AND TIPS
Fairly well-drained soil, in either sun or part shade.	Bedding plants will be readily available, or sow seeds in a heated propagator between late spring and mid-summer for flowering the following year.	• Remove faded flowers regularly to encourage new ones to form. • Pomponette Mixed is a pretty mixture to raise from seed. It is particularly compact and has strong colours.
Any reasonable soil, including alkaline or chalky, in sun or part shade.	Available as plants, or sow seeds outdoors between mid-spring and early summer. Pinch out growing tips when plants are 7.5–10cm (3–4in) tall.	• Pinch out the shoot tips of young plants to encourage good, bushy growth. • The delicate perfume of wallflowers will attract bees into the garden. • Try growing them with tulips in strong colours.
Choose a sunny spot with well-drained soil.	Plant the bulb-like corms as soon as they are available, usually in autumn. Planting depth varies with corm size, but generally 7.5–13cm (3–5in).	• Crocuses look best planted in miniature drifts, randomly spaced to look natural. • Try naturalizing crocuses on a grassy bank. Instead of making individual holes, lift sections of turf, plant corms into the soil beneath and replace.
Moist yet well-drained soil, in dappled shade or sun.	Buy either as pot-grown plants or tubers. Plant preferably in late summer or early autumn, placing tubers 2.5–5cm (1–2in) below the soil surface.	• Apply leafmould or garden compost every autumn to keep soil in good condition. • Cyclamens are often collected from the wild, damaging native habitats in the process. Check that yours are from a cultivated source.
Fairly well-drained soil, in sun, part shade or shade.	Soak the wizened-looking tubers in tepid water for a few hours before planting. The foliage dies down in summer, so always interplant with summer flowers.	• If you have problems establishing winter aconites from tubers, specialist nurseries sometimes supply them "in the green" (plants lifted shortly after flowering whilst still in leaf). Although more expensive, these are generally easier to get started.
Will tolerate a wide range of soils, in part shade or, ideally, full sun.	Best planted in spring or autumn. Incorporate leafmould or garden compost on planting to ensure that the soil doesn't get too dry. Water in dry weather.	• After flowering, trim lightly to keep plants really dense and compact. • As ground cover, they look best planted in groups of several plants of the same colour, odd numbers if possible.
Choose any spot in shade with reasonable soil, not too damp nor too dry.	Plant the bulbs in early autumn – at least 10cm (4in) deep – in miniature drifts under trees and shrubs. When clumps become congested, lift and divide.	• If establishing snowdrops from bulbs proves tricky, obtain them "in the green" (just after flowering and still in leaf) from a specialist nursery. Check that snowdrops sold as bulbs have not been collected from the wild.
Well-drained soil, in plenty of sun.	Plant the bulbs as soon as they become available in garden centres and nurseries (early to mid-autumn) at a depth of 15–23cm (6–9in).	• To encourage a good show the following year, feed with a high-potash fertilizer every two or three weeks as soon as the flowers start to fade. • Choose one of the many named varieties for variations in colour.
Well-drained yet moisture-retentive soil, in dappled shade.	Plant the bulbs as soon as they are available, usually in autumn, at a depth of 5–10cm (2–4in). They thrive on being left where they are for years.	• Deadheading prolongs the flowering period. • To keep them flowering well, make sure that the soil is neither boggy nor allowed to become too dry. • Congested clumps can be divided for more plants.
Must have a sunny spot with free-draining soil, ideally chalky.	Best planted in spring or autumn. Incorporate grit into the soil to improve drainage. Species can be raised from seed, but named varieties will not come true.	• Deadheading helps to prolong the flowering period; towards the end, leave some of the fluffy seedheads on the plant to enjoy. • I love 'Rubra' (rich red), 'Alba' (white) and 'Barton's Pink' (delicate shell pink).

COLD COMFORT
The courageous little winter aconite flowers in the chilliest winter. Its silky golden petals stand proud even in snow.

TAMED SPIRITS
Although you may shun its wild relatives, *Bellis perennis* – here Tasso Series – is a great plant for containers or borders from early spring onwards.

Flower markings just like little sparkling eyes

A LA MODE
There are many varieties of *Iris reticulata* available, in a range of striking shades – this is 'J. S. Dijt', in regal purple. Add them to spring containers for their richness of colour and elegant form. Some have a subtle yet distinct perfume.

Late summer and autumn flowers

ALL TOO OFTEN, FLOWER borders come to a crashing halt by late summer – everything starts to look tired and sorry for itself. By adding some late-season performers to your garden, you can keep colour and brightness going well into autumn and so prolong the life of your display.

OTHER LATE-SEASON FLOWERS

Perennial asters (*Aster*) pp.78–9
Coreopsis (*Coreopsis*) pp.138–9
Gazanias (*Gazania*) pp.140–1
Rock roses (*Helianthemum*) pp.138–9
Penstemons (*Penstemon*) pp.34–5
Rudbeckias (*Rudbeckia*) pp.88–9

AUTUMN COLOUR
The long, trumpet-shaped, fiery flowers of *Crocosmia*, packed along elegant stems, bring true autumn warmth to beds and borders. Fans of sword-shaped leaves in bright green make a vivid contrast.

Compact buds open into star-shaped flowers

PASTEL POWER
Large, flattened heads of minute flowers, usually in shades of pink, sit above the cool, pale, succulent leaves of *Sedum spectabile*. On warm days they are covered with butterflies and bees.

PLANT	SIZE	APPEARANCE
JAPANESE ANEMONES *Anemone × hybrida, A. hupehensis*	H 75–150cm (30–60in) S 45–60cm (18–24in)	For late summer and autumn flowering performance, these hardy herbaceous anemones are difficult to beat. Their shell-like petals, usually in white, pink or lilac-pink, surround a circle of golden stamens.
Chrysanthemum	H 45–90cm (18–36in) S 30–45cm (12–18in)	Think rich, think showy – chrysanthemums are both, and more! From late summer into early autumn these mostly half-hardy herbaceous perennials are a blaze of golds, bronzes, yellows, oranges, pinks and reds.
AUTUMN-FLOWERING COLCHICUMS *Colchicum*	H 15–25cm (6–10in) S 10–15cm (4–6in)	Picture an alpine meadow in autumn, and there will be colchicums, studding the turf with large, goblet-shaped flowers in white or lilac. These hardy corms are perfect for naturalizing in grass or for underplanting.
MONTBRETIAS *Crocosmia*	H 45–90cm (18–36in) S 10–15cm (4–6in)	The fiery reds, oranges and yellows of autumn foliage are captured in the funnel-shaped flowers of montbretias, carried on arching spikes. These hardy corms bloom in late summer and early autumn.
CONEFLOWERS *Echinacea purpurea*	H 90–150cm (3–5ft) S 50cm (20in)	These daisy-like flowers in white, pink or purple are an excellent foil for more exuberant late-flowering plants. Hardy herbaceous perennials, they are a late-season treat for bees and butterflies.
HELENIUMS *Helenium*	H 90–120cm (3–4ft) S 30–40cm (12–16in)	A clump or two of these cheerful daisy-flowered perennials, in warm shades of red, yellow or brown, will brighten any border late in the season. As with coneflowers, each bloom has a prominent raised centre.
DAYLILIES *Hemerocallis*	H 60–90cm (2–3ft) S 30–45cm (12–18in)	These mainly hardy, evergreen perennials bloom in profusion during late summer. The flamboyant, trumpet-shaped flowers come in dazzling hues of pink, orange, yellow, red, wine or plain white.
NERINES *Nerine bowdenii*	H 45cm (18in) S 30cm (12in)	The elegant, fragile, spidery-looking trumpet flowers of these perennials are grouped into loose heads. The pink, delicately scented flowers look exotic, but nerines are remarkably hardy.
KAFFIR LILIES *Schizostylis coccinea*	H 60cm (2ft) S 25–30cm (10–12in)	These hardy perennials produce showy, star-shaped flowers on loose spires from late summer until mid-autumn. Flowers come in bright red, pink or white and the leaves are bright green, sword-shaped.
ICE PLANTS *Sedum spectabile*	H 40–45cm (16–18in) S 40–45cm (16–18in)	In late summer, tiny, starry, usually pink flowers with near-purple centres are grouped into dense, rounded flowerheads on these hardy herbaceous perennials. The leaves are succulent and a greyish-blue.

SITE	CULTIVATION	HINTS AND TIPS
Prefer a moist yet well-drained soil, in part shade or full sun.	Best planted in spring or early summer. Add organic matter before planting, and mulch before the hottest weather to keep the roots cool and moist.	• For best flowering, grow in part shade. • In the first season after planting or in extremely cold areas, protect the crowns over winter. • Divide in spring or take cuttings from sturdy roots in summer (see p.41).
Select a sunny position with well-drained, well-fed soil.	Plant in spring, once any late frosts are over. If the soil is poor, incorporate well-rotted garden compost on planting. Provide support for tall varieties.	• When all flowers and leaves have faded, cut the stems back to 10–15cm (4–6in) above soil level and cover the crowns with a mulch 10cm (4in) deep. In very cold or wet areas, cut back, lift the entire plant and store in a cool greenhouse.
Choose a partly shaded, sheltered spot with well-drained soil.	Plant corms in groups, about 10cm (4in) deep. Incorporate some fertilizer if the soil is poor. Keep them well watered in periods of dry weather.	• Don't let the soil dry out in summer, or flowering will be reduced. • The leaves can become quite large, so avoid planting colchicums where they can smother smaller plants in spring.
Well-fed, well-drained, moist soil in either full sun or part shade.	Plant corms in groups in late winter or early spring, about 10–15cm (4–6in) apart. Propagate by dividing established clumps every few years in spring.	• Cut back faded flower spikes promptly to encourage good flowering the following year. • Keep well watered in dry weather. • Severe winters can damage them, so mulch with a deep layer of chipped bark or similar material.
Choose a sunny spot with any reasonably well-drained soil.	Best planted in spring and autumn. Propagate by dividing established plants in spring or autumn, or take root cuttings (see p.41) in early spring.	• Plant taller types at the back of the border, and provide support if necessary. • Pick the variety 'Robert Bloom' for deep purple-red flowers, or 'White Swan' for white blooms with a hint of green.
Best in a sunny spot with reasonably moist soil.	Plant in autumn or early spring. Incorporate organic matter to encourage the soil to hold moisture. Divide established clumps in autumn or spring.	• If you deadhead after the first flush of flowers fade, a later flush will often develop. • Taller heleniums will need some support. • Group several plants of the same variety for a really rich, colourful display.
Reasonably moist soil, in sun.	Best planted in spring or autumn. Daylilies are easy to grow, although they may take a year to reach their full potential. Consider mulching in dry sites.	• Clumps lose vigour after about four years, so divide them and replant the more vigorous sections in late summer or early spring. • Choose herbaceous daylilies in frost-prone climates; the evergreen types are tender.
Well-drained soil, in full sun, ideally close to a warm wall.	Best planted in spring. In cold areas, protect over winter with a deep layer of chipped bark, or plant in containers that can be sheltered.	• Nerines dislike being disturbed, so leave them alone as long as possible. Divide very congested clumps in late summer so that they have time to re-establish before winter. • N. bowdenii is the only species that survives frost.
Moist but not soggy soil, in sun or part shade.	Best planted in autumn or spring. Keep the soil moist at all times or flowering will be badly affected. Every fourth year, divide congested clumps in spring.	• Although hardy, in severe winters or cold areas it's safest to mulch the crowns with a deep layer of chipped bark or similar material. • Exciting varieties are 'Major' (crimson), 'Maiden's Blush' (pink) and 'Viscountess Byng' (bright red).
Choose a sunny spot; the soil must not be too heavy or wet.	Ideally, plant in autumn or spring. Leave the dead flowerheads at the end of the season – they help to protect the crowns over winter.	• Other early- and mid-autumn-flowering sedums well worth growing are 'Ruby Glow' (reddish-purple flowers), 'Autumn Joy' (pink, reddening with age), which will thrive in a shady spot, and 'Bertram Anderson' (red).

LATE LUXURIANCE
Packed to bursting with colour, heleniums are joined by solidagos, achillea, bergamots and roses – proof that the end of summer can still mean bright borders!

HIGH IMPACT *below*
Japanese anemones such as this *Anemone hupehensis* 'September Charm' bring colour and height to a late summer or autumn planting.

Flowers with fantastic foliage

WITH MANY FLOWERING plants, the blooms hog the limelight, but with these, superb foliage competes with the flowers for top billing in your garden, with the added bonus that it lasts longer. When not in flower, their leaves will provide a foil for other plants in bloom.

OTHER FLOWERS WITH FANTASTIC FOLIAGE

Aquilegias (*Aquilegia*) pp.94–5
Corydalis (*Corydalis*) pp.144–5
Cyclamens (*Cyclamen coum*) pp.154–5
Euphorbias (*Euphorbia*) pp.52–3
Geraniums (*Geranium*) pp.120–1
Yuccas (*Yucca filamentosa*) pp.140–1

TEXTURE AND TONE *right*
I'm fascinated by the metallic sheen to the leaves of *Heuchera* 'Pewter Moon'. Their under-surfaces are just as striking, in a bold, rich pink.

LEAFY LARGESSE *left*
The large, prominently veined foliage of hostas – here 'Tall Boy' – gives a lush effect. In late summer, this is complemented by masses of pale purple funnel-shaped flowers.

PLANT	SIZE	APPEARANCE
BUGLES *Ajuga reptans*	H 10–25cm (4–10in) S 45cm (18in)	In no time at all, bugles form a dense mat of evergreen foliage with, depending on the variety, purple, reddish or variegated leaves. Dense, bright blue or purple flower spikes develop in spring and into early summer.
LADY'S MANTLE *Alchemilla mollis*	H 50–60cm (20–24in) S 75–80cm (30–32in)	The rounded, lobed, serrated leaves are slightly downy, and greyish-green beneath lime-green flowerheads. Forming a lovely mound of erect stems, this perennial looks pretty sparkling with raindrops or dew.
CORAL FLOWERS *Heuchera*	H 25–45cm (10–18in) S 20–30cm (8–12in)	The tiny flowers on tall stems that develop in early summer are held above a clump of beautifully coloured or patterned leaves. These hardy perennials often retain most of their foliage throughout the year.
HOSTAS *Hosta*	H 30–60cm (12–24in) S 45–90cm (18–36in)	Magnificent foliage – mainly broad, rounded leaves in lime green, blue-green or silvery-blue, often with yellow, cream or white variegation – earns these hardy perennials a place in almost any garden.
DEADNETTLES *Lamium maculatum*	H 20–30cm (8–12in) S 30–60cm (12–24in)	The attractive silver- or white-splashed leaves on these hardy perennials usually look good all year round. They make good ground cover. Pretty flower spikes in white, pink or red-purple appear in summer.
LUNGWORTS *Pulmonaria*	H 25–30cm (10–12in) S 45–60cm (18–24in)	Although these hardy herbaceous perennials produce pretty purple, red, pink, white or blue flowers in spring, their foliage provides interest all season, with white or silver patterning on dark green.
LONDON PRIDE *Saxifraga × urbium*	H 20–25cm (8–10in) S 60cm (2ft)	This hardy perennial holds its tiny star-shaped flowers above unusual rosettes of bright green foliage. The flowers, held in loose heads, appear in early summer and are white with pink markings.
HOUSELEEKS *Sempervivum*	H 5–7.5cm (2–3in) S 25–35cm (10–14in)	These evergreen succulents form spreading, textural rosettes made up of numerous fleshy, pointed leaves packed tightly together in green and red. Pink flowers on tall fleshy stems appear in summer.
PICK-A-BACK PLANT *Tolmiea menziesii*	H 60cm (2ft) S 30cm (12in)	The common name refers to the fact that young plants are formed on mature leaves, pick-a-back style. An evergreen perennial, it forms a mat of rounded, slightly crinkle-edged, pale green foliage.
VARIEGATED PERIWINKLE *Vinca major* 'Variegata'	H 30cm (12in) S 90cm (3ft)	The arching stems on this hardy perennial are covered in pale green leaves with pale yellow margins. Throughout mid- and late spring they are studded with extremely pretty pale purple-blue flowers.

SITE	CULTIVATION	HINTS AND TIPS
Any moist soil, in sun or shade.	Best planted in spring or autumn. Create new plants by separating off the tiny plants that form on self-rooted stems, or divide in spring or autumn.	• Clipping off early flower spikes when faded may encourage plants to flower into autumn. • I particularly like 'Braunherz' (shiny, dark purple-brown leaves) and 'Burgundy Glow' (with white or pinky-red variegation on green).
Very easy to please. Grows in sun or shade and in all but very wet soils.	Ideally, plant in autumn or spring. Propagate by moving tiny plants that have self-seeded to the desired position, or divide clumps in spring or autumn.	• Lady's mantle is easy to grow and readily self-seeds, sometimes to the point of nuisance! • Useful as a gap-filler in almost every conceivable place. Try planting (or letting them self-seed) in the spaces between large paving slabs.
Any moist soil, in sun or part shade.	Best planted in autumn or spring. An annual mulch with leafmould or well-rotted compost keeps growth looking healthy and lush.	• Plants can be divided every couple of years in early autumn. • One of my favourites is 'Pewter Moon', which has purple leaves with distinctive silvery-grey marbling on the upper surface.
Most moisture-retentive soils are suitable, in sun, shade or dappled shade.	Autumn or spring are the best times to plant. An annual mulch of leafmould or garden compost helps the soil to remain moist.	• Established clumps can be divided in late summer or early spring. • Slugs and snails are a problem, so be prepared to do battle with these pests. Hostas planted in pots fare better, but keep them well watered.
Well-drained soil, in anything but deep shade.	Best planted in autumn or spring. Trim after flowering to keep their dense shape. If they become invasive, divide in autumn or spring.	• Deadnettles bring dry, shaded areas beneath trees and larger shrubs to life. • Pretty varieties are 'Beacon Silver' (pure silver leaves), 'White Nancy' (silver with green edges) and 'Pink Pewter' (pale green with a silvery sheen).
They thrive in reasonably moist soil, in dappled or full shade.	Ideally, plant in autumn or spring. To keep the plants in top condition, water during dry spells and remove faded flowers. Divide mature plants in autumn.	• In relatively mild climates lungworts may retain their foliage all year. Pick off any deteriorating leaves, which may attract fungal infections. • For leaves that are silver all over, look out for varieties such as *P. saccharata* 'Argentea'.
Needs moist or damp soil with partial shade.	Best planted in autumn or spring. If the soil is not sufficiently moist, add bulky organic matter to aid moisture retention.	• Obtain new plants by separating off individual rosettes with roots from established clumps in autumn or spring. This is also a good way of tidying specimens that have begun to look moth-eaten; replant only the vigorous parts of each plant.
Choose a sunny spot with well-drained, light soil.	Late spring or early summer are the best times to plant. Add plenty of grit if your soil is not very free-draining. Separate off rosettes with roots as new plants.	• Their succulent leaves enable houseleeks to withstand drought better than most plants grown for lush foliage. • Once a rosette has flowered it dies, but will be replaced by new ones growing around the parent.
Moist, preferably acid soil, in full or dappled shade.	Best planted in autumn or early spring. Keep plants well watered if the soil gets the slightest bit dry. A mulch helps to preserve moisture in the soil.	• Increase stocks by removing and potting on the tiny plants that are produced on the leaves. • For really gorgeous cream- and yellow-blotched leaves, choose 'Variegata' or 'Taff's Gold'. • A useful plant for ground cover.
Well-drained soil, in part shade or sun.	Ideally, plant in autumn or spring. Propagate by removing rooted stems in autumn or spring. Alternatively, divide established clumps in spring.	• Will grow in quite dense shade, but may lose some of its variegation and flower less profusely. • An annual mulch after thorough watering helps the plant to thrive on soils that tend to get dry. • If it starts to spread too much, cut back in spring.

VERDANT VELVET
The finely toothed, slightly furry leaves of *Alchemilla mollis* look as if they have been cut from a gorgeous, pale green velvet.

LONGTIME COMPANIONS
I've grown lungworts in every garden I've had. Here, *Pulmonaria saccharata* 'Frühlingshimmel' shows off its silvery foliage and blue flowers.

RAINBOW AT YOUR FEET
The crinkly, creeping foliage of bugles makes good ground cover; for the most striking leaf patterns, choose *Ajuga reptans* 'Multicolor'.

Flowers for ground cover

PLANTS FOR GROUND cover are too often associated in people's minds with the boring, low-maintenance greenery used in car parks. Not so! All the plants I have chosen here will create a carpet that scores points for both foliage and flowers, as well as helping to suppress weeds.

OTHER FLOWERS FOR GROUND COVER

Bugles (*Ajuga reptans*) pp.158−9
Elephant's ears (*Bergenia*) pp.144−5
Campanulas (*Campanula*) pp.96−7

Geraniums (*Geranium*) pp.120−1
Deadnettles (*Lamium maculatum*) pp.158−9
Periwinkle (*Vinca major*) pp.158−9

CLOUD NINE *right*
The handsome form of *Tiarella cordifolia* means that plants look equally good grown singly as when used as ground cover.

VINTAGE BLUE *left and below*
Like little blue pyramids, the flowerheads of *Muscari armeniacum* − commonly known as grape hyacinth − do look very much like upside-down bunches of grapes.

PLANT	SIZE	APPEARANCE
ROCK CRESS *Arabis*	H 20−25cm (8−10in) S 50−60cm (20−24in)	Forms a dense, grey-green carpet of foliage covered in small white or pink flowers from mid-spring to early summer. The flowers of these hardy evergreen perennials are held in spikes that get taller as they age.
AUBRETIA *Aubrieta deltoidea*	H 15−20cm (6−8in) S 60cm (2ft)	Although small, the flowers are so plentiful and their colours so rich that they make a huge impact in spring, especially planted in groups. The foliage of this hardy evergreen perennial is covered in very short hairs.
MOUNTAIN AVENS *Dryas × suendermannii*	H 20cm (8in) S 60cm (2ft)	This hardy perennial creates an evergreen carpet of tiny leaves similar in shape to oak leaves. From late spring until mid-summer, gorgeous nodding white flowers with bright yellow stamens appear.
BLUEBELLS *Hyacinthoides non-scripta*	H 25−30cm (10−12in) S 15cm (6in)	There is no more glorious sight in late spring than trees in bud standing in a sea of bluebells. The flower spikes of these hardy bulbs are draped with miniature hanging bells in white, a deep, rich blue, or pale pink.
GRAPE HYACINTHS *Muscari*	H 10−20cm (4−8in) S 10−15cm (4−6in)	In spring these hardy bulbs produce dense, almost conical spikes of tiny blue or white flowers, with a slight fragrance. The leaves are greyish-green and narrow. Try growing under shrubs in miniature drifts.
KNOTWEED *Persicaria bistorta* 'Superba'	H 90cm (3ft) S 60cm (2ft)	Shaped like prettily coloured bottle brushes, dense, bright pink flower spikes are produced above mounds of light green foliage from late spring to mid-summer. A perennial, it is semi-evergreen.
FRINGE CUPS *Tellima grandiflora*	H 80cm (32in) S 60cm (2ft)	This hardy herbaceous perennial thrives in cool, shaded situations. Its foliage is light green, rounded and lobed, and flower spikes of tiny, yellowish-green bells appear from late spring until early summer.
FOAM FLOWER *Tiarella cordifolia*	H 15cm (6in) S 45cm (18in)	Like waves of white froth, loose flower spikes of tiny, star-shaped, creamy-white flowers waft above the pale green, lobed foliage in summer. This hardy perennial forms an attractive evergreen carpet.
NASTURTIUMS *Tropaeolum majus*	H 20−30cm (8−10in) S 20−30cm (8−10in)	These hardy annuals produce a fiery display of large, open flowers throughout the summer. The leaves, bluish-green, are nearly circular. Varieties are available in cream, yellow, orange and reddish-orange.
LESSER PERIWINKLE *Vinca minor*	H 20cm (8in) S 75cm (30in)	This hardy evergreen perennial is grown for its long, trailing stems that break out in pretty pink, white or bluish-purple flowers from spring until early summer. Variegated forms are available.

SITE	CULTIVATION	HINTS AND TIPS
Well-drained soil, in plenty of sun.	Best planted in spring. Once most of the flowers have faded, trim the plant with shears to keep it bushy. Plants can be divided as soon as flowering is over.	• Rock cress will grow in both a fairly heavy soil and in shade, but the foliage will be less dense and flowering less prolific. • For interesting variegated foliage with distinct pale yellow leaf margins, try 'Variegata'.
Well-drained, preferably alkaline soil and plenty of sun.	Ideally, plant in spring. They will grow better in alkaline soils or in slightly acid soils that have been limed first. Divide plants in late summer.	• Once flowering is over, you can give plants a "haircut" with shears to keep them compact. • If the plants start to look patchy, divide in late summer and replant vigorous sections only. • Ideal for planting in gaps in stone walls.
Needs free-draining, preferably acid soil and plenty of sun.	Spring is the best time for planting. Add extra grit and acidic material such as chopped bracken to improve the drainage and acidity of the soil if needed.	• Take semi-ripe cuttings in summer. • Leave the faded flowers on the plants to allow the attractive, silky seedheads to develop. • This is a small-scale ground-cover plant for use with other small plants – try it amongst alpines.
A moist but not soggy spot, in dappled shade.	Best planted about 13–15cm (5–6in) deep, as soon as the bulbs are available in late summer. Self-seeds readily, but takes 5 years to grow into flowering bulbs.	• Allow bulbs to naturalize and form drifts beneath groups of trees. Choose the smaller-flowered forms for a more natural effect. • Bluebells can multiply to the point where they become a nuisance, so beware of them in borders.
Choose a sunny spot with reasonably well-drained soil.	Plant the bulbs 5–7.5cm (2–3in) deep in late summer or autumn. They are very easy to please and need little care. Divide established clumps every few years.	• Unusual edging for paths or borders, but they are invasive and may outgrow their welcome. • They look great in containers and windowboxes. • They will grow fairly well in part shade, but will flower less profusely.
Thrives in moist but well-drained soil, in sun or part shade.	Best planted in autumn or spring. Regular watering is advisable, at least until it establishes; subsequent growth will be much more rapid.	• Divide established clumps in autumn or spring. • Will do quite well in shade, where flowers and foliage both tend to be rather paler in colour. • The flowers of knotweed make unusual cut flowers that last well.
Well-drained but moist soil, in a cool spot in dappled shade.	Ideally, plant in autumn or spring. Divide established clumps in autumn or spring to rejuvenate them.	• Water regularly if there is any danger of the soil drying out; this is particularly important when the plants are establishing. • In severe winters or very cold gardens, provide winter protection.
Cool, moisture-retentive, ideally acid soil, in partial shade.	Best planted in autumn or spring, incorporating leafmould to improve soil texture if necessary. Divide established plants in autumn or spring.	• Planted beneath trees and shrubs, foam flowers make particularly pretty ground cover. • This foam flower has a creeping habit and will gradually develop a spread of close to 90cm (3ft). • In winter the foliage turns an attractive brown.
Well-drained soil, in full sun.	They dislike too dry a soil, so add organic matter if the soil is light. Sow seed in a heated propagator in spring. Harden off, then plant out after any late frosts.	• Plant them 20–25cm (8–10in) apart to make good ground cover on a sunny site. • Nasturtiums also make great container plants. Water regularly so that they don't get dry, and don't overfeed them or they will not flower.
Any reasonably well-drained soil, in full sun or part shade.	Best planted in autumn or spring. If the soil tends to dry out, add bulky organic matter at planting. Mulching will also help strong growth as plants establish.	• It grows quickly and if planted at 60cm (2ft) intervals will soon form good ground cover. • To increase your plant stocks, sever and replant those stems that have formed their own root systems.

VARIATIONS ON A THEME
Most nasturtiums have plain green foliage, but for interest even when not flower try this variegated form, *Tropaeolum majus* 'Alaska'.

REFORMED CHARACTER
The mere mention of knotweed fills most gardeners with fear, but this cultivated form, *Periscaria bistorta* 'Superba', looks good and is easy to control.

CHARM SCHOOL
Like other rock cress, this rich pink *Arabis blepharophylla* 'Spring Charm' is equally useful growing in rock gardens and borders. I also love to see it planted in gaps in a stone wall.

Glossary

Words in *italics* within a definition have a separate entry.

ANNUAL A plant that completes its life cycle (growing from seed, flowering, setting seed and dying) within one year.

BACKFILL Replace soil or soil mix around roots after planting.

BEDDING PLANT Plants (usually *annuals*, but sometimes *biennials* and *perennials*) that are used for temporary, often showy, display.

BIENNIAL A plant that produces leafy growth in the first year and then flowers, sets seed and dies the next.

BRACT A modified leaf at the base of a flower or flower cluster. Bracts may resemble normal leaves or be reduced and scale-like in appearance; they are often large and brightly coloured.

BULB A group of swollen, modified, underground leaves that act as a storage organ.

COMPOST An organic material resulting from the rotting down of organic material from the kitchen and garden. Also a prepared growing medium available in different forms, for example multi-purpose compost, cuttings compost and seed compost.

CORM An underground, bulb-like, swollen stem or stem base.

CROWN The part of a *herbaceous plant* where the stems meet the roots and from where new shoots develop.

CUTTING A piece of stem, root or leaf that, if taken at the correct time of year and prepared and cared for in the correct way, will grow to form a new plant. Basal stem cutting: one taken from the base of a (usually *herbaceous*) plant as it begins to produce growth in spring. Root cutting: one taken from part of a semi-mature or mature root. Semi-ripe cutting: one taken from half-ripened wood during the growing season. Softwood cutting: one taken from young, immature growth during the growing season.

DEADHEADING The removal of spent flowers or flowerheads so as to promote further growth or flowering, prevent seeding or improve appearance.

DIVISION The lifting and dividing of a plant clump into small pieces, which are then replanted.

DWARF Naturally small-growing mutation of a plant, often vegetatively propagated to produce a named dwarf variety.

f. (*forma*, form) Applied to plants within a species that differ in some minor character.

GENUS A group of related species linked by common characters, e.g. *Digitalis* (foxgloves).

HALF-HARDY Not able to withstand frost.

HARDY Able to withstand frost and cold and therefore grow outside throughout the year.

HERBACEOUS PLANT One with top-growth that is soft, not woody, and (usually) dies back over winter.

HYBRID The offspring of genetically different parents, usually of distinct *species*.

LEAFMOULD Fibrous, flaky material derived from decomposed leaves, used as an ingredient in potting composts and as a soil improver.

MULCH A material applied in a layer to the soil surface to suppress weeds, conserve moisture, and maintain a cool, even root temperature. In addition to organic materials such as manure, bark and garden compost, polythene, foil and gravel may also be used.

NAMED VARIETY See *variety*.

PERENNIAL A plant, usually *herbaceous*, that lives for at least three years.

POTTING ON Transferring a plant from a small pot to a larger one.

POTTING UP Transferring seedlings into individual pots of compost.

PROPAGATOR A covered tray that provides a humid atmosphere for raising seedlings, or other plants being propagated. Some have an electrical heating element in the base.

RHIZOME A swollen stem that grows horizontally, producing roots and shoots.

SEED A ripened, fertilized ovule containing a dormant embryo capable of developing into an adult plant.

SPECIES A category in plant classification within a *genus*, denoting closely related similar plants.

SUBSP. (subspecies) A subdivision of a species, higher in rank than *varietas* or *forma*.

TUBER A thickened, usually underground, storage organ.

VAR. (*varietas*, variety) Naturally occurring variant of a wild species, perhaps with a different flower colour.

VARIETY A cultivated variety of a plant as distinct from a wild, naturally occurring variant, also known as a "cultivar".

VARIEGATED Marked with one or more colours. Often used to describe leaves with white, yellow or cream markings.

X Sign denoting a *hybrid*.

Index

Where there are several references, the main entries are indicated in **bold**.
References in *italics* refer to illustrations. Where the common and Latin plant names
are the same, only the Latin name is used.

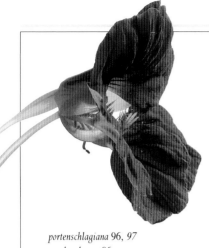

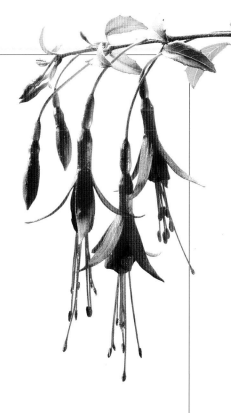

Acknowledgments

AUTHOR'S ACKNOWLEDGMENTS
My thanks to Jenny Jones, Jane Bull, Annabel Morgan, Louise Abbott, Lee Griffiths, David Lamb, Anne-Marie Bulat and everyone else at Dorling Kindersley for their help and enthusiasm in putting this book together, to Dave King for his fantastic photographs, and to Alasdair, who carried on with everything, including the digging, once "the bump" had got too big.

PUBLISHER'S ACKNOWLEDGMENTS
Editorial assistance: Diana Vowles, Tanis Smith. Additional DTP design: Sonia Charbonnier.
Overseas liaison: Alison Rich. Index: Ella Skene.

WE EXTEND SPECIAL THANKS TO THE FOLLOWING GARDEN CENTRES FOR THEIR HELP:
Forest Lodge Garden Centre
Holt Pound, Farnham, Surrey GU10 4LD
Hopleys Plants Ltd
Much Hadham, Herts SG10 6BU
Kelways Ltd
Langport, Somerset TA10 9EZ

PICTURE CREDITS
The publisher would like to thank the following for their kind permission to reproduce their photographs:

a=above; c=centre; b=below; l=left; r=right; t=top

A-Z BOTANICAL LTD: D W Bevan 26cr. HEATHER ANGEL: 36cl. BRUCE COLEMAN COLLECTION: Kim Taylor 10tl. MELANIE ECLARE: 41c, 48–49, 60br, 61c. THE GARDEN PICTURE LIBRARY: Brian Carter 86br; Kathy Charlton 141cr; Ron Evans 128–129; John Ferro Sims 11bc, 67cr; John Glover 12c, 84cl, 120br, 126tl, 127tr; Juliet Greene 82c; Marijke Heuff 103tr; Michael Howes 112br; Jacqui Hurst 57c, 69bl; Lamontagne 11br; Mayer/Le Scanff 2, 85bl, 102c, 103tl; Jerry Pavia 63tl; Howard Rice 11c, 13tc, 30-31, 42b, 114cr; J S Sira 94br; Juliette Wade 46tr, 99tl; Didier Willery 111br, 118crb; Steven Wooster 47br, 64–65, 71tc, 129tr, 157tr. JOHN GLOVER PHOTOGRAPHY: 26br, 34bc, 63tr, 72br, 74cr, 90–91, 93br, 97br, 113c, 120. JERRY HARPUR: 33tl, 39tc, 40l, 54cl, 55br, 76–77, 78bl, 88br, 97tr, 104br, 119bl, 125tr, 129 (garden designed by Simon Hopkinson). SANDRA HYTCH: 5tr, 58c, 122–123. ANDREW LAWSON: 6–7, 12cl, 12–13, 13tr, 35, 40cl, 45tc, 53, 54cr, 59bl, 66c, 68cl, 81tr, 92cl (Brook Cottage, Alkerton), 94cl, 94cr, 97c, 109tr, 111tr, 115bl, 124bl, 126clb, bc, 126–127, 127br, 128tl, bl, c, 132cl, 154 cl. CLIVE NICHOLS: 37tc (Sticky Wicket, Dorset), 38r, 50bl (Bassibones Farm, Bucks.), 57tl (Vale End, Surrey), 68tr, 73c, 101cl (Greystone Cottage, Oxon.), 112tr, 118cl, c, cr, 134 cl, 135 tr, 144cl (Greystone Cottage, Oxon.). PHOTOS HORTICULTURAL: 27bl. PICTOR INTERNATIONAL: 129tc. HOWARD RICE: 79bl, 95. TIM SANDALL: 27c & r. JULIETTE WADE: 72cr.

JACKET: MELANIE ECLARE: back tcl; front bc; inside front bc. THE GARDEN PICTURE LIBRARY: Howard Rice back tr. JOHN GLOVER: back bl, front bl, tr. JERRY HARPUR: back tl, front tcl. ANDREW LAWSON: back br; inside front br; spine t. CLIVE NICHOLS: front tl, br.